KIRSTIE ALLSOPP

INTRODUCTION
p.7

THE
VINTAGE HOME
p.11

VINTAGE
STYLE GUIDE
p.31

VINTAGE FURNITURE
p.53

SOFT FURNISHINGS

p. 93

FINISHING TOUCHES

p. 139

VINTAGE CELEBRATIONS

p. 185

CONTACT LIST *p. 214*

INDEX *p. 218*

ACKNOWLEDGEMENTS *p. 221*

INTRODUCTION

If you don't love the place where you live, everything suffers. In this book I want to teach people who have lost their way how to turn their houses into treasured homes.

'Past and craft' is a mantra that I've lived by for years, and one that I'm determined to spread. I want to inspire people to reuse, recycle, make do and mend, ditch the factory-made for the handmade, and delve deep for vintage finds. Forget the new – bring in the old!

For the TV series *Kirstie's Vintage Home* I set up my own vintage workshop in a café on the bohemian Portobello Road in London. I crammed it with a wide range of skilled designers and makers, and made it my one-stop shop for everything handmade and homespun. The experts shared their crafting skills with me so that I, in turn, can share them with you. Among the many projects and techniques in this book, I'll be showing you how to turn neglected items into beautiful design pieces, and how to create heirlooms that can be passed on to children and grandchildren. Above all, I want to show you how to take inspiration from different decades of interior design – from the glamour of the art deco era to the pop art colours of the 1950s.

While I am not an interior designer, property has always been my thing. I suppose I would call myself a true believer in the home. I am convinced that the key to creating interiors we love is to personalise our homes with unique items that reflect us. And the two best ways to do this? Looking to the past, to items that are pre-loved, worn in and ripe for reinvention or reuse, plus making personal and unique items by crafting them ourselves.

Looking to the past to furnish and decorate your home has become a very trendy way of doing things in recent times. Vintage is 'in', but as far as I am concerned, it's the only way to make a house a home. Long after the fashion crowd are onto the next thing, I will still be trekking around second-hand shops and antiques markets. I hope that by the end of this book you'll be just as hooked as I am.

The best bit about shopping, buying and thinking this way is that everything holds a history. Once you get into this mindset, believe me, there is no going back. It's like an addiction and you are always on the lookout for your next fix. It's all about seeing the potential in items, and that's where the second part of making a home comes in – craft.

If you want to inject personality, warmth and comfort into your home, there is no better way to do so than by making something with your own hands. If you haven't done so already, I'd urge you to discover the joy — and addictiveness — of crafting. You'll end up with something unique that nobody else in the whole world has, something special you can pass on to future generations.

Crafting for the home doesn't have to be complex, and it certainly doesn't have to be perfect. There are endless straightforward, effective and simple projects around, and this book has some of them. So if you are new to the crafting game, start small, perhaps with some cushions, and build up to more complicated things. And if a seam is a bit wonky or a fabric pattern doesn't match up exactly, then hey, who would really notice anyway?

Ultimately, my message is this: the past and crafts go hand in hand because they're both about seeing the potential in things for your home and giving them a new lease of life. Whether it's painting an old chair, displaying vintage tins or making cushions from period fabric, if you surround yourself with things you love, you are creating a beautiful home that reflects who you are and what you are all about.

THE
VINTAGE HOME

VINTAGE. Everyone's talking about it, but why is vintage so great? Well, the reason I truly love it is because it has a history. Vintage things have been cared for and loved through generations. They've stood the test of time and, once you get your hands on them, they will continue to be cherished for many years to come.

WHAT IS VINTAGE?

Nowadays the word 'vintage' is bandied about all over the place, especially in relation to style and fashion, but I think it's just a smart way of saying second-hand. Of course, *The Oxford English Dictionary* gives a slightly more elevated definition, saying that vintage 'denotes something from the past of high quality, especially something representing the best of its kind', so let's use that as starting point. Furniture, soft furnishings, crockery, china, absolutely anything for the home can be vintage if you're not the first person to have owned it, though it must be from the past and less than a hundred years old — any older makes it antique.

Vintage items have an inherent attractiveness and charm about them. I think of them as having personality and wearing their heart on their sleeve because of their visible wear and tear. That is something you simply can't recreate, no matter how hard you try.

In auction rooms up and down the country, you will find old furniture that is beautifully designed, built and finished. It's generally true to say that if you buy vintage, you're buying something worthwhile, but not all vintage items will be looking their best when you first clap eyes on them in a shop window or auction house. More often than not, you have to look closely to see the potential. Could some cleaning and polishing turn a sad item into something desirable, or would painting and perhaps replacing fabric or handles be more in order? A little elbow grease and imagination can work wonders, and in this book I'm giving you lots of ideas and techniques for returning vintage items to their former glory. With these in mind, I hope you will be encouraged to look past the grime and see the gorgeousness.

My home is kitted out from top to bottom with wonderful second-hand finds. I don't have a specific period that I stick to when shopping; I am more eclectic in my purchases, and simply buy things that I take a fancy to. It makes me happy to live with things I find pleasing and that are totally personal to me. Your home should do this for you too.

The best thing about creating your own vintage home is that it will be completely personal to you. You're never going to walk into a friend's living room and see the same identikit furniture and furnishings if you've handpicked individual vintage items. Of course, achieving the look is going to take a bit of effort – it's not something you can find in a shop catalogue and buy wholesale – but you can have so much fun putting it together. The look is built up over time through finding things you like, things you think are beautiful, and sometimes even things you think are ugly but that can be worked into your scheme in some way. It comes about by finding a mish-mash of pieces for your home that can include cheap second-hand furniture you do up yourself, more expensive original items, pre-loved family pieces (valuable or not), one-off auction wins, and items that you have crafted yourself.

Clearly, vintage interiors take time and commitment, but what an interesting and satisfying time you will have creating yours! This book will guide and, I hope, inspire you on your way, whether you're after a specific period style or a mix and match of styles. I will take you through each stage of the process – planning your home (page 25), buying and doing up furniture (page 53), making and arranging soft furnishings (page 93) and finally crafting and adding those extra special finishing touches (page 139).

During the course of the TV series, six different families were helped to create the vintage era of their dreams in their homes, and the results were just amazing. The homes were wonderfully stylish but still eminently practical, and that's as it should be. My Vintage Style Guide on page 31 will show you how the families' dreams were achieved, and you can use them as inspiration for your own dream vintage look.

MERGING OLD AND NEW

It's important to make the point here that vintage style for your home is not about historical re-creation of rooms from the past. I'm definitely not suggesting that we travel back in time. A house decorated from top to bottom in a 1930s' style, for example, could very easily look staid and feel more like a museum than a home. Our homes have to reflect the fact that we live in a modern world, otherwise they will be completely impractical. It's all about taking the best from bygone eras and adding your own modern twist.

The trick to creating a successful vintage style is merging old and new. Sounds easy, but how do you actually go about this? To my mind, it's about

combining vintage pieces with items you already own (even if you need to do a bit of work on them to make them fit in), plus mixing in what you really need to live. For example, if you have a modern fitted kitchen but you love the 1950s' look, you could invest in a vintage Formica-topped table to start your theme, using the bright colours from the table to guide your colour choices for walls and window treatments. You could then add other authentic 1950s' touches, such as a 'molecule and atoms' coat rack (very popular in homes of the time), or three plaster ducks flying up the wall (ubiquitous in houses of that era). Finally, you could match your modern appliances in similar colours to bring the look together.

A note about buying new: if you do need to buy something new for your home, I urge you to buy British wherever possible and support our wonderful British designers and makers. After all, they are making the vintage items of the future. I believe that new designs can be life-enhancing too, so I'm all for mixing it up. The other week, for example, when my potato masher broke, I bought a modern one with an innovative handle design. It's much more comfortable to use and makes the smoothest mash ever. Even better is that it's fully designed and made in Britain.

WHY BUY VINTAGE?

I'm a vintage shopaholic and I'm proud of it. There are lots of reasons why vintage shopping is so addictive, but the most important one for me is that it's an emotional experience, not just a monetary transaction. I fall in love with objects and can't leave without buying them. Of course, you never know when this is going to happen because you can't go with a precise shopping list and you never know what you are going to find. Vintage buying is more about finding a connection to a piece and wanting passionately to spend time with it in your home. You never settle for second best when you're second-hand shopping. Believe me, once you start you won't be able to stop.

Second-hand shopping for me is not just a preference, it's a statement of belief. I think it's absolutely essential that we all start buying second-hand and continue buying second-hand because we simply can't go on manufacturing new things in the way we do and filling up landfill sites with the old stuff that we don't want any more. Second-hand needs to become a way of life. On a recent trip to the USA I was amazed and impressed that 'yard sales' take place every weekend all over the country. Americans believe that one person's trash

Opposite: *A pretty display of vintage glassware in Amber and Colin's 1960s-style bedroom.*

is someone else's treasure. We need to get into this mindset. Things don't have to be brand new and never used before to be new to us. Our world just doesn't have enough room for us all to buy this way all of the time.

Buying second-hand also offers real value for money – it's cheaper! If any reason to buy second-hand is going to get you, surely this is it. I wager that any piece of furniture you pick up in an auction room will almost certainly cost less than buying it from a shop. Of course it's easy to go to the local flat-pack furniture shop and pick up take-away furnishings, but it really isn't any cheaper than shopping at auctions, markets, junk shops, salvage yards and second-hand shops. Those flat-packed items also lack the passion and attention to detail that talented craftspeople put into their work. Buy second-hand and you are getting something that will last and won't need to be replaced a year down the line.

LET'S GO SHOPPING!

I'm on the lookout for vintage items at all times because you just never know what you might come across when you're out and about. There are the traditional places, such as car boot sales, charity shops, junk shops, auction houses, markets, and reclamation and salvage yards. Then you've got specialist vintage and antique shops, and the Internet is great too for both specialist and non-specialist buys.

Not knowing what you are going to find doesn't mean you can't do any preparation for your shopping trip. In fact, I strongly recommend you plan out your rooms and draw up a wishlist. This is especially helpful when you are buying furniture. If you have the dimensions of your rooms with you at all times, you'll never be stuck when you come across a piece of furniture that you love and want to check whether it will fit. (See page 22 for advice on planning your furniture and what to look for when you shop.)

Similarly, if there is a colour scheme that you want to follow, or a pattern that is setting the style of your room, carry a colour chart or pattern swatch with you at all times so that you can guarantee what you are buying will fit with your scheme. (Pages 98–100 offers lots more ideas about soft furnishings.)

AUCTION HOUSES
My favourite place to buy second-hand is at auction houses. I'm the daughter of an auctioneer, so what do you expect? My ongoing mission is to get each and every person in the UK into our wonderful auction houses. Don't be afraid.

Opposite: *From the ancient and decrepit to the pretty and colourful, you can find virtually any object of your desire in antiques houses and markets.*

They can seem like daunting places from the outside, but once you go in and learn how they operate, they are the friendliest, most wonderful places to be, and they hold a treasure trove of vintage items.

If you haven't been to an auction house before, just tell the staff who work there that it's your first time, and they will show you the ropes and hold your hand throughout the process. Without customers they can't exist, so they're happy to help.

The great thing nowadays about auction houses is that they publish their catalogues online. Often you can put in an early bid for something if you can't attend the auction itself, or you can browse the catalogue before you head along so that you know exactly what you want to bid on. If you can find the time to go along regularly to your local auction house, I urge you to do so because there's always a bargain to be had.

Many people assume that buying at auctions takes a lot of time, but I want to dispel that myth once and for all. Not long ago, my family and I were spending the day in Exeter, so we popped into the local auction house to look around the pre-sale. After just an hour's browsing, we left our bids and checked in later that week to see what we had won. From that one short browse I picked up a birthday present for my dad, plus the prettiest jug with six matching glasses, all for a bargain price. It couldn't have been quicker or easier.

Visiting auction houses – and second-hand shopping in general – is a wonderful recreational activity for all the family. My kids love rummaging among the goodies on offer and, in case you're wondering, they have never broken anything. Instead they go around absolutely fascinated, seeing things they would never otherwise come across, and asking, 'What is this? Where does it come from? What's it made of?' It's really educational. Just the other week my goddaughter picked up a vinyl record and asked what it was because she had never seen such an old-fashioned thing in her home. It made me feel very old.

One last word about buying at auction: consider buying job lots. This is where an assortment of stuff is sold off in a box, and you get the entire contents. The jug and glasses that I won in Exeter were part of a job lot that I paid £20 for, but the glassware alone was worth that to me, so I was happy with my purchase. It turned out that my friend liked a vase from the box, so she took that, and my other half took a large bowl that I didn't like (I have to admit it looked OK once he had put some things into it), so everyone was happy.

INTERNET

Knowledge is power, and the Internet provides both if you use it efficiently. First, it can help you to research the price of second-hand items, and then you can use that knowledge to bargain more confidently. Of course, prices fluctuate according to changing fashions, but knowing the going rate is really useful when it comes to haggling. (See page 60 for more on vintage furniture trends.)

Lots of dealers in vintage and antique items buy and sell online – in fact, some do almost all their business on the Internet. Their sites are especially valuable if you are looking for a specific item, so do a search and see what pops up. Some, for a fee, will also track down items on your behalf, which is useful if you've set your heart on something and your own searches have drawn a blank. Specialist sites are also great resources if you are a collector.

I collect Allsopp Beer memorabilia, as it makes great presents for my family. It's fairly hard to come by, although I do find the occasional thing at markets and in second-hand shops. I regularly check into the big auction sites, such as ebay.co.uk and uk.ebid.net, and I suggest you do the same. If you have the time and you really want something, check in every day and look out for new things coming on. Although auction sites are popular with private sellers, lots of specialist vintage stores sell through them too.

When buying from auction sites, the rule is haggle, haggle, haggle. Look for the 'Buy it now' price, then click on the 'Make an offer' button just below it and make an offer. This can produce great results, but if you are a collector or want something specific, you might find it difficult to drive a hard bargain in case you miss out on the item altogether. In that case, I'd advise you not to worry about sometimes paying over the odds for items that you really, really want. If they mean that much to you, the price is worth paying.

The drawback of buying online is that you can't touch and feel the things you want to buy. The only solution is to check the description carefully so that you know exactly what you are getting. Amber and Colin, who were doing up their 1960s' Edinburgh pad, found a fantastic vintage sideboard online and were willing to take the risk of buying without seeing it in person. The gamble paid off, and they got a piece that really finished off their room. My best advice is always to get as much information as possible about the seller and the item they are selling. Under the Sale of Goods Act, what you buy must be 'as described', 'of satisfactory quality' or 'fit for purpose'. When buying from auction sites, remember that your contract is with the seller, who is often a private individual, not with the auction site itself, so thoroughly check their returns policy before you do the deal.

SECOND-HAND MARKETS AND SHOPS

As with all second-hand shopping, it's possible to spend lots of time at markets but still leave empty handed because there is nothing that really takes your fancy (although that never seems to happen to me). My best advice is to take your time when you're browsing and have a good rummage around. Remember that most things can be cleaned up and polished, or sanded down and painted.

I took Iman, who was getting his home ready for the imminent arrival of his new baby, to Newbury Market, and he bought an amazing array of stuff. Among them was an art deco-style wooden letter holder and a 1930s-style table lamp, both perfect for the art deco living room that he and his wife Heather had in mind. A mirror and a fire-screen completed the trip – all picked up at bargain prices, and unique items never to be found elsewhere.

RECLAMATION AND SALVAGE YARDS

Ever wondered where old banisters, fireplaces, chandeliers and other big discarded items end up? The answer is reclamation yards and salvage yards. It's possible to find almost anything in these places, from vintage parquet flooring to pretty knick-knacks (our families found a whole range of stuff), though nothing will be in tip-top shape or ready to use. If you are looking for large-ish vintage items and are willing to put in the elbow grease to get them looking good and back in working order, these yards are the place to go.

I took Ellie and Nick, who were doing up their house in Kent, to my favourite reclamation yard in Park Royal, west London. They found a whole table's worth of items for their 1930s' kitchen and dining room, including light fittings, door handles, vintage signs, picture frames, baskets, an old iron and an unusual knife cleaner. And because they were buying so much, they were able to negotiate on price and bagged themselves a bargain.

SKIPS

If someone is getting rid of something, the chances are that they won't mind you taking it, but the law states that you must ask the owner's permission first. Recently my other half and I were driving home and spotted the most beautiful French doors in a skip around the corner from our house. There didn't seem to be anyone around to ask permission, so we went for it. Hours later a friend called asking where her French doors were. She had spotted us manhandling them up the street on her way back from the shops, but we hadn't noticed the number of the house the skip was outside. Fortunately, she didn't mind, but if you find yourself in a similar situation, don't get caught out – always ask.

Opposite: *Lovely old picture frames, and often lovely old pictures, can be found in markets and junk shops if you delve deep enough.*

Kirstie's
VINTAGE SHOPPING GUIDE

When you're shopping for vintage there are four main pieces of advice that I can give you. I've learnt them over the years and to me they are invaluable. Always have them at the forefront of your mind when second-hand shopping and you won't go too far wrong. Here goes...

1.

Don't worry what others think. It's your home and you are the one who has to look at the item every day. If you like it, go for it. Have confidence in your taste and what you love. I always take a leaf out of my kids' book because they have none of our inhibitions when it comes to second-hand shopping. Kids really don't have a sense that something isn't good if it's second-hand. If they like it, they don't care what others think. Be a proud forager.

2.

Be decisive. When I was at a market recently, I spotted a tin bath that I thought would be great down at Meadowgate for washing wellington boots outside the back door after muddy jaunts through the woods. Foolishly, I decided to have a think about it, and guess what? I was beaten to it and missed out. If you've done your planning, you'll always be carrying your wishlist of items and it will help you to be decisive when you spot something (see page 25 for more about this).

3.

Remember, almost anything can be washed. Hot soapy water can go a long way towards making something look or smell a whole lot better. If you're considering an upholstered item, give it a good sniff and then judge whether you should buy it. You can get a really great bargain on a second-hand bed, for example, but I know lots of people turn their noses up at the very idea. I've noticed that beds often seem to have been hardly used, so I reckon it's definitely worth checking them out. Use your judgement: if you can see that something has happened on the bed (the mind boggles), don't buy it; but if it smells and looks all right, there's nothing stopping you.

4.

Don't be afraid to negotiate. My son collects paperweights and whenever he spots one at a market, he will walk right up and ask how much it costs. No messing about, he gets straight to the point. The other week he did just that and the vendor told him the price was £4. What did he do? He pulled all the money he had out of his pocket (a grand total of £2.20) and offered that. What did the vendor do? Sold it to him. My son was honest, upfront and knew what he wanted – an example well worth following. Always pay what you think the item is worth to you.

10 STEPS TO
PLANNING A ROOM

Before you hit the shops or start getting handy with the mouse, you need to do some thinking and planning. This takes time, but it's well worth it. Have a notebook, pencil, measuring tape and ruler at the ready.

1 . **Assess the space you have.** Stand in the middle of the room and take a 360-degree look around. If you were to strip all the stuff out, what would be left? What are its assets? Does it have large windows? Which direction does the room face, and when does it get the best light? Are there any features, such as fireplaces or alcoves? Take note of all the positives in the room that you might want to accentuate. Similarly, note down the negatives. Is there anything you'd like to cover up or disguise? Are the windows small? Do you need to find a way of bringing in more light? Try to be objective and look at the room with fresh eyes.

2 . **Think about your lifestyle and how you use the room.** What activities does it need to accommodate? Do you watch television here? Do you need an area for a hobby or for eating? How should the space work for you? What doesn't work for you currently in the room? If you have kids, a living room will work differently than if you live on your own and work from home, for example.

3 . **Measure the room and draw out a floor plan of the space,** preferably to scale on graph paper. Make a note of all the dimensions, including height, and plot out the doors, windows and any features. This will help you to get a better sense of how the room could be organised.

4 . **Think about the furniture.** What have you got already? What would you like to keep? Could any of the current furniture potentially be reinvented or revitalised with a paint job? Don't be too quick to discard what you already have – you may well have a vintage treasure right under your nose. Do any of the items suggest a vintage era or a look you could go for? Jot down all your existing pieces of furniture in a notebook, then think about any extras you need to make the room function properly. Don't try to cram in too much; the room will ultimately dictate what you can buy. No matter how hard you try, a large kitchen dresser, for example, just isn't going to fit in a galley kitchen.

Opposite: *This is a great example of a room that cleverly mixes vintage pieces from different eras while remaining practical and making good use of the space available.*

Take a look around other rooms in the house and see if there are any items that would be worth swapping around. Also double-check in your loft or garage that there isn't a long-forgotten chair of your granny's that you could dust down and paint for a 1950s-inspired living room, or an old desk from your student days that could be reworked with veneers for a 1970s-style home office.

5. **Plan out different options.** Make multiple copies of your floor plan and plot out ideas of where the furniture you have might sit. Depending on the size of your room, there will almost certainly be different ways to configure it. Use this exercise as a way to start planning what else you need to buy, and what size or style of other furniture would work in the space.

6. **Think about soft furnishings.** What do you already have in the room? Is there a rug or a set of curtains you love? Do you have, for example, a piece of 1920s' fabric that could be your starting point? What do you want to change? What is needed?

   Similarly, is there something from another space that could be reworked? If, for instance, you love the colour and pattern of some curtains discarded from your mother's house, could you take them apart and re-sew them into a bedspread and cushions? I've done this sort of thing many a time.

7. **Are you keeping the existing colour scheme?** Do you need to repaint? Would wallpaper work instead? Do any items of furniture or soft furnishing have a colour or pattern that you love and could use as inspiration? If so, make sure you always keep relevant swatches in your bag, along with your notebook and floorplan, when you go on your shopping trips. Mixed patterns and colours can look great in a room, so don't feel you have to stick to just one. Pick colours that tone together, then mix the patterns, connecting them through colour. This will give the room a sense of unity. (See page 94 for more about soft furnishings.)

8. **Don't forget the lighting:** it's a key element in setting the tone of any room. Note down where the main overhead light is, but never use it as your main light source – it's too harsh to be relaxing. You need multiple light sources in a room to create an ambient feeling, and you definitely don't want any dark corners. Where are the sockets for plugging in table and floor lamps? Where are the tables to put lamps on? What lamps do you already have? Is there room for a floor lamp?

9. Please don't neglect the walls after you have chosen paint or wallpaper. Do you really want to view blank spaces whenever you sit down to relax? No! Think what you want your walls to say about you. What are you interested in? How can the walls reflect that? If a stranger stood in the room and regarded your walls, what would they learn about you? You'd surely want them to think you're more than a blank.

10. Is there a particular vintage period you'd like your home to reflect? If so, do some research. What features were typical of that time? Which elements of it do you love and want to bring into your home? What furniture is key to creating the look? What soft furnishings and colours were popular? What objects would help to set the tone? Don't be afraid to group items made from different materials. Wood and plastic, for example, can be authentically mixed together in rooms inspired by several different eras.

For further information about particular looks, see pages 31–51 and discover how the families in the TV series created their vintage homes with my Vintage Style Guide. But also bear in mind that second-hand shopping is unpredictable and occasionally your well-laid plans will go clean out of the window.

HOW TO DEVELOP YOUR VINTAGE STYLE

It's all very well collecting and shopping for second-hand things you love, but making them work together is a whole different ball game.

First, don't panic or feel that you need to get everything at once. Decorating and making your house a home is a gradual process, so don't expect vintage heaven overnight. It's taken me years of committed shopping and hunting to get the house I have today. Setting your own personal style is all about layering your home with things year in, year out, adding to and constantly evolving its appearance. It's only by doing this that you can create somewhere that is yours and yours alone.

Don't let anything into your home that you don't absolutely love, or at least ensure it has the potential to be turned into something you love. When deciding what to do with a room, consider what you would want on those four walls if you had to live with the result forever. What could you bear to look at till the

end of your days? Sounds dramatic, but maybe we should all live by this rule if we really want our home to be our own special haven.

Janine and Shaun, for example, wanted a bedroom full of romance and elegance. The sophistication of *fin de siècle* (a late nineteenth-century style) was obviously a perfect way to achieve it, so we went with the flow and used a subdued palette of dove greys, blues and florals. We then created a flowing canopy to drape over the bed, added customised bedside cabinets and incorporated lots of mirrors. The results were truly romantic (see page 132).

Take your time and play musical chairs with your furniture, soft furnishings and knick-knacks. It's a great way to freshen up rooms. I'm not suggesting you should move your wardrobe or sofa every week, but occasionally rearranging ornaments or pictures can give you a new perspective on everything else. These small moves can give a room a new lease of life, and might spark other ideas, such as how to display a collection or where an extra chair might fit.

Once you have started to build up a few items that you love, set them down together in one room and see if a theme is emerging. Have you gone for similar colours or patterns? Are there particular items that combine well? Is there an item of furniture that could benefit from some renovation and maybe set the style? Could you pretty things up with a bit of crafting to help bring the room together? If you do spot a theme, whatever it is, that is a good place to start. Ellie and Nick had a beautiful collection of pastel-coloured pottery, and Ellie runs her own company making vintage-inspired homeware in duck egg colours, so we used both of these as inspiration for their 1930s' country kitchen. Alongside this, they already had a wonderful dresser, which became the focal point of the room and added to the overall theme. These three key things – pottery, homewares and dresser – inspired all their crafting and shopping choices for the rest of their makeover. (See page 50 for more about creating your own mood and inspiration board.)

Of course, there's a real art to making beautiful displays of all your collections, photographs and pictures, but practice makes perfect. Gather similar items together, perhaps grouping them by colour or style. A collection of candlesticks, for example, could be arranged in varying heights on a shelf or windowsill, while a collection of letter openers might be better mounted in a frame that can be leant against the back of a shelf. The memory box on page 90 shows how to make a simple but very effective display of family heirlooms, and the Finishing Touches chapter (see page 139) offers lots more ideas. Whatever you love, there is a way of making it work as part of your home.

Opposite: *Does combining vintage pieces get any better than this? Three different eras – baroque, 1920s and 1960s – are cleverly united by their curves and colours, and brilliantly complemented by the zebra-skin rug.*

In my television series *Kirstie's Vintage Home* I helped families who wanted to turn their houses into homes. Busy lives, young families and hectic careers had taken their toll, and a combination of clutter, disorganisation, unfocused shopping, collecting and hoarding did nothing to help matters.

I wanted to show these families that by taking design inspiration from the past, crafting and sourcing original period pieces, they could make a home they were proud of – somewhere they could have friends round without any embarrassment, and, most importantly, a home in which they could relax and be themselves. They all put in the hard graft needed to transform their rooms, and the results changed their lives – for the better and forever.

In each property we used a different era as inspiration. Nobody was aiming for historical perfection; instead they were going for a practical, modern home with a vintage twist, using colours, designs, crafts and features from their chosen period.

I've put together a guide to those eras, focusing on the rooms I helped transform in the series. It's not comprehensive, but I hope it might help to give you a flavour of each period along with the key design trends. Use it to spark ideas and to put your own spin on your vintage look.

TWENTIETH-CENTURY HOMES

At the turn of the twentieth century, the average household in Britain contained 4.65 people because families were usually large, with four or five children. The majority of the population lived in cities and towns, working in factories and living in overcrowded housing built by the factory owners.

Few properties had running water or an inside toilet. People did all their cooking on a coal-fired range that also heated the house. The kitchen was the hub of the home. The front room, usually kept for 'best', was where people entertained. Upstairs the unheated bedrooms were dimly lit because people didn't trust the gas lighting. As for personal hygiene, people bathed once a week in front of the range and had stand-up washes in between.

Over the course of the century, the way we lived our lives was transformed. A rise in income, coupled with innovative ideas for making life more comfortable, helped change the domestic scene beyond recognition. When gas cookers were introduced in the 1920s, people no longer had the range to huddle around for warmth, so they left the kitchen and moved through to the living room, where they gathered beside the fire, which was as likely to be gas as coal.

Electricity also came into our homes during the 1920s and 1930s, and altered the way we used them. It gave us brighter, cleaner lighting for hobbies and reading, allowed the use of new technologies and also brought about a change in interior design (see page 37).

The 1950s and 1960s saw the spread of many labour-saving devices, such as vacuum cleaners and fridges, when mass production brought their prices down. Suddenly, mundane domestic chores became easier. Inside toilets became the norm by the 1960s, and central heating became commonplace in the 1970s.

By the end of the twentieth century, the average household size had almost halved. Now there were just 2.4 people per dwelling, and house building had vastly expanded; we were moving out to the suburbs in our droves. Where there had been 7 million permanent homes in 1900, now there were 22 million. And in England, where a mere 10 per cent of people owned their own home in 1914, an astonishing 68 per cent did so by 1999.

Design flourished during the twentieth century, and Britain produced some of the most talented designers in the world, all of whom contributed to making our lives more efficient, sustainable and enjoyable.

The upshot is that we now have more time away from domestic chores, more space to ourselves, and more money to spend on making our homes look good.

THE 1920s

The start of the 1920s was an optimistic time. People wanted to leave the trauma and horror of the First World War behind and begin a new decade of hope, peace and prosperity. Living standards were relatively high, so people rebuilt their lives and the economy prospered.

During the mid-1920s the government introduced subsidies to encourage house building. This, coupled with advances in construction technology, saw a building boom that continued well into the 1930s. Where there had been 8 million houses in 1919, there were over 12 million by 1939. The new houses, mainly semis and detached properties, were built on rural land around already established towns, and thus the suburbs were born.

In terms of style, no single definitive look prevailed in the 1920s. However, a 1925 exhibition in Paris brought the art deco movement to the world, and this had a huge global influence.

Art deco is an opulent decorative style characterised by rounded corners, streamlined angular shapes and geometric patterns. Its influences came from the industrial world of mass production and commercialism. Recurring motifs include sunbursts, cruise liners, aeroplanes and cars, which appeared on everything from garden gates to personal stationery. They symbolised speed and the dawn of a new technological era.

New materials were embraced by this new look. Chrome was heavily used, as was steel (which was also being used to make new skyscrapers). Plastics, such as Bakelite, were invented at this time and remained popular throughout the period.

Furniture was made in exotic and expensive hardwoods, such as ebony and teak, which were easy to sculpt and bend into art deco shapes and motifs. For people of more limited means, lots of furniture was made with cheaper wood that was covered with hardwood veneers.

After the discovery of Tutankhamun's tomb in 1922, Egyptian influences made their mark on art deco. Pyramids, zigzags and black cats became all the rage on decorative surfaces, and jungle animal prints were popularised by those who went on African safaris (admittedly, only the wealthy).

Art deco permeated all aspects of design in the late 1920s. It led to beautiful typefaces, such as Gill Sans (1926) and those used in the titles of Fred Astaire films. It could also be seen in architecture, such as the Savoy Hotel in London.

IMAN AND HEATHER'S ART DECO LIVING ROOM

Among those who contributed to *Kirstie's Vintage Home* were Iman and Heather, who wanted to draw on art deco style to transform their living room from a blank canvas into a wonderfully opulent space. Having travelled extensively throughout Sri Lanka, Kenya, China and India, they wanted to include these influences too – all perfect for an art deco look.

Authentic art deco colour schemes are bold, often black and white, but the style can also incorporate pastel shades. Think ice cream colours, such as pink, peach, pale blue and beige. Iman and Heather kept a neutral base with shades of white and cream, and added accents of gold and orange in their accessories and soft furnishings. Perhaps their boldest period statement was a cowhide rug with a sepia zebra print. It was a great way to add the art deco style. You could do this too and save on the expense of changing the whole floor.

Opposite: *Art deco was a very opulent style, with lots of shiny surfaces and streamlined shapes. The type of room shown here provided inspiration for Iman and Heather's art deco project.*

For lighting, choose curved lamps, shades and wall lights to echo the period. When I took Iman shopping at Newbury Antiques Fair, he bought a beautiful 1930s-style table lamp with curved lines and a glass shade – perfectly art deco.

Mirrors and glass are a must in any art deco scheme, and a starburst mirror should be top of your shopping list. For even more opulence, add accessories that incorporate shiny elements, such as enamel and mother-of-pearl. Iman found a beautiful curved wooden letter holder that fitted the bill. I also learnt gold leaf gilding with Adam Williamson (see page 177) to make some lavish-looking picture frames that echoed one of the accent colours in the art deco room.

For a finishing touch to an art deco scheme, you can't do better than add some Bakelite, a form of plastic that was popular at the time for light switches, telephones, radios and a host of ornaments and knick-knacks. Keep your eyes peeled in junk shops and auction houses – you'll easily find some Bakelite bits, and they won't cost much either.

THE 1930s

After the high of the 1920s, the Great Depression hit the UK in the 1930s, and by the end of that decade we were at war again. It was a period of contrasts because, despite a worldwide depression, a decline in traditional industries and high unemployment, prices fell faster than wages, meaning that money was actually worth more. That is, if you were lucky enough to have a job and money to spend.

The consumer society we take for granted today was born in the 1930s, and hire purchase brought a range of fancy new home appliances within the reach of many more people. Other luxuries also became available (car ownership increased in the first half of the decade), and new entertainment came our way too (the 'talkies' arrived in 1927, and cinema attendance boomed during the 1930s). Home ownership, promoted as a moral good for family life and Britishness, continued to rise in this unstable era, as did the exodus to the suburbs that had started in the 1920s.

The room that saw the biggest changes during the 1930s was the kitchen. In new suburban homes kichens now had efficient plumbing, were fitted with electric lights and boasted modern gas stoves. It was domestic heaven!

Opposite: *This lovely 1930s' room has the curved shapes typical of that decade, and even an early television set in the corner.*

ELLIE AND NICK'S 1930s' KITCHEN/DINER

When Ellie and Nick came to me in despair about their neglected kitchen and dining space, we decided to embrace the period look of the 1930s in their new design, but with a modern twist.

In the 1930s, kitchens weren't fitted, cupboards often had curtains instead of doors, and the floor was covered with lino. If you love this look, it's easy to recreate. Lay down a retro floor covering, find a 1930s' fabric, such as a small floral print, for your cupboard curtains, and display crockery and utensils on open shelves and dressers to stay in keeping with the period look.

Ellie and Nick already had a lovely pine dresser, so we put it in their dining area and used it to display their wonderful collection of pottery. They also bought old plate racks and hooks from salvage yards to store other items.

Colours typically used during the 1930s were pale because clean electricity replaced smoky gaslight and did away with the need for dark tones to disguise the grime. With this in mind, Ellie and Nick chose a gentle colour scheme based around duck egg blues and pastel greens, inspired by their pottery collection.

Handicrafts were hugely popular in the 1920s and 1930s, and magazines such as *Woman's Weekly* published a steady stream of home craft patterns and ideas. Inspired by this, Ellie and Nick made a lino-cut blind for their kitchen (see page 124 for how to do this).

No 1930s' kitchen would have been complete without a ceramic butler's sink, ideally overlooking the garden so that the housewife could keep an eye on her children. It was likely to be surrounded by tiles, another key feature of kitchens at the time. To emulate this look, I showed Ellie and Nick how to put up handmade tiles above their cooker (see page 167).

To give their kitchen its finishing flourishes, Ellie and Nick sourced vintage utensils in enamel (very popular in the 1930s) and displayed them with their pottery, which included hand-moulded plates we made together (see page 160). At Ray Cullop's salvage yard, they picked up vintage signs, an old iron and a knife cleaner, and displaying these things really added an authentic finishing touch to their rooms.

Opposite: *Ellie and Nick's kitchen/diner was given a rustic style and dressed with 1930s' vintage elements, such as wicker baskets, willow placemats and enamel jugs.*

THE 1950s

After the black-out and restrictions of the Second World War, the 1950s were a much brighter time. Although rationing was still in place at the start of the decade, just a few years later wages had increased and the British economy was growing. We were all more affluent and had more disposable income. Our horizons were expanding, and more people started going on foreign holidays (the first jet plane was produced in Britain in 1954).

Technology stepped up its infiltration of our homes. In 1953 the Post Office issued roughly 3 million television licences, and about 27 million people crowded around friends' and neighbours' sets to watch the coronation of Queen Elizabeth II, an average of nine people per set. By the end of the decade, 16 million households had televisions, and it was possible to watch in a bit more comfort. In addition, more appliances (such as automatic washing machines, fridges and food mixers) had begun to creep into our kitchens.

The Festival of Britain in 1951 was designed as a 'tonic to the nation', intended to improve morale and help us forget the trauma of war. At multiple locations around the country it celebrated Britain's history, achievements and culture, and was a huge showcase for home-grown design, architecture and art.

JANINE AND SHAUN'S 1950s' FAMILY ROOM

When Janine and Shaun wanted a makeover for their home, they opted for a 1950s' look and feel, so I helped them to recreate that era in the redesign of their family playroom-cum-craftroom.

Innovations in paint technology during the 1950s meant that the dark colours of the 1940s (usually applied by professionals because they were difficult to work with) could be abandoned and we could all buy off-the-shelf vinyl paint and do it ourselves (the 1950s was the supreme age of DIY). Janine and Shaun took colour inspiration for their room from their stunning green period tea set. Using the green as a starting point, they painted and distressed dining room chairs in a variety of bright colours that reflected the optimistic feeling of the time (see page 66 for this technique). Bright pinks, greens, blues, yellows and purples are all absolutely authentic for a 1950s' scheme.

Once the chairs were dry, they were upholstered with a gorgeous, 1950s-inspired floral fabric (see page 115). When it comes to fabrics of this period, the choice is very diverse – either bright, bold florals or abstract patterns inspired by advances in science (think starbursts and atoms), so look out for these too.

Opposite: *Shaun and Janine's playroom-cum-craftroom after its 1950s' makeover.*

Inevitably, furniture changed too in the post-war years. Whilst 1940s' sofas had bulky frames stuffed with hessian and horsehair, those produced in the 1950s benefited from innovations in both techniques and materials. New ways of working with wood allowed designs with light frames, sleek lines and elegant shapes. Scandinavian furniture, with its minimal adornment, was particularly popular. Janine and Shaun got a steal on a typical mid-century sideboard at a salvage yard, and they also sourced an original 1950s' kitchen unit online, which they adapted for storage in their playroom.

For an authentic 1950s' look, juxtapose wooden furniture with plastic, Formica and chrome, all popular materials at the time. Alternatively, source an original basket-weave chair, or a hi-tech butterfly chair (a metal frame with fabric hung over it) to complete the look.

For finishing touches, Janine and Shaun picked up vintage craft signs, postcards and other knick-knacks. While not all came from the 1950s, they cleverly mixed and matched to make them look related. Other items that say '1950s' are magazine racks and coat racks that incorporate bright plastic balls on the legs or hooks, examples of atomic-age design from the Festival of Britain. Janine also picked up some brilliant crochet rugs at car boot sales for a tenner each. They were just like the ones a 1950s' housewife might have made, and proved how useful it is to keep your eyes open for anything that might finish off your scheme. It's definitely the little extras that make all the difference.

Opposite: *Interior design enjoyed an explosion of colour during the 1950s – a reaction to the subdued palette of the war years. Furniture became lighter, sleeker and generally more fun.*

THE 1960s

Huge changes came about in the 1960s. Society, particularly the younger generation, was rebelling, experimenting and challenging conventions. Attitudes from previous decades were being thrown out, and Britain was becoming a more liberal, less restricted and truly vibrant society. Parent power gave way to a youth culture – the swinging sixties had arrived!

Music became faster and louder – the Beatles leapt to fame in 1962; art became bolder and more colourful – think Andy Warhol and Pop Art; and fashion brought us the mini skirt. It was the space age – by 1969 the USA had put the first man on the moon; it was a nuclear age – the Cuban missile crisis erupted in 1962; and it was an age of supersonic travel – *Concorde* took its first flight in 1969. These examples are the very tip of the iceberg in terms of changes and developments that took place over this short period. Suffice to say, the way we lived changed forever.

Across society as a whole, the average income was rising, so people had more money to spend. The younger generation could now afford to leave home and set up on their own. The time was ripe for mass-produced furniture. Good design at low prices became within the reach of everyone when Habitat opened its doors in 1964, but the DIY surge that had started in the 1950s continued to grow (B&Q opened its first store in 1969). Flatpack furniture was also a 1960s' phenomenon (not everything from that decade was great).

Open-plan living became all the rage. In houses everywhere, walls were knocked down to combine sitting room, dining room and kitchen into one large space. The fitted kitchen gained popularity. Inevitably, the way we used our homes started to change. Habits became more flexible and informal – eating, living and entertaining all happened in the same large room.

Some commentators claim that the 1960s was the pinnacle of interior design because there was so much experimentation and change, which still exerts an influence on designs today. Designers were looking at old forms in new ways, and dreaming up new ones with the latest advances in plastic and metals. Some took the lines and stylised flower shapes of art nouveau and twisted them into psychedelic styles. Others went on the hippy trail to places such as India and Morocco and incorporated ethnic influences from those countries into their designs. Still others looked to the future, creating a space-age style. As a result, there is no single defining look for the 1960s.

Opposite: The British love affair with bold colours continued into the 1960s, and furniture was now influenced by the space age. Just look at those amazing 'flying saucer' floor cushions!

AMBER AND COLIN'S 1960s' SITTING ROOM AND BEDROOM

It was great fun helping Amber and Colin to return their 1960s' seaside maisonette to its roots. It had typically clean, unfussy lines and they wanted the interior to reflect the period. They adore the music from that time, which is when their parents met, so it was all adding up.

Amber and Colin love rainbows (their daughter even has Rainbow as a middle name), so a colourful palette was used to reflect this. If you're going for a 1960s' look, you could choose vibrant clashing colours, toning complementary colours, or even psychedelic ones – anything goes in a 1960s' scheme. In their sitting room Amber and Colin opted for neutral walls, floor and sofas, using them as a backdrop for vintage fabrics in a range of colours, textures and patterns, and choosing red as an accent colour, which was picked up by the rug. The reupholstered ottoman (see page 74) continued the theme very successfully.

In the bedroom, the couple went for a boldly patterned wallpaper (very much in vogue during the 1960s). A beautiful handmade quilt (see page 108 to make your own) provided both complementary and contrasting colours.

In terms of furniture, the sitting room coffee table was a 1960s' classic, its curves and spherical lines certainly influenced by the space age. After much online searching, Amber also sourced a beautiful sideboard at a bargain price. This we customised and brought bang up to date by screen-printing a design onto it (see page 80 if you'd like to do this yourself). Another great find was an original 1960s' shelving unit, which was used to display vintage finds and hand-crafted pieces, such as spray-painted vases and letters (see page152). Wooden furniture often lived alongside plastic in 1960s' homes (chairs, for example, were often made from plastic), so don't be afraid to mix and match these materials in your scheme.

For lighting, Amber and Colin chose a spherical, space-agey lampshade, but could also have gone for a classic paper lantern (a great look that has never gone out of fashion). On the desk they had another timeless classic – an Anglepoise lamp. Of course, there are lots of other lighting options. If you want to introduce a touch of psychedelia to your 1960s' scheme, why not incorporate a lava lamp? And for an authentic ethnic influence, you could dot your room with Moroccan lanterns made of prettily punched-out metal. All can be found online, or search at auctions and second-hand markets.

The crowning glory of the room was a sunburst mirror – very popular during the 1960s. You might be lucky and pick one up second-hand. If not, see the Contact List on page 216.

Opposite: *Amber and Colin's sitting room is a fantastic space, full of 1960s' panache.*

THE 1970s

The 1970s saw the liberal attitudes of the 1960s increasingly embraced by the mainstream, but the British economy took a downward turn. Inflation went through the roof, industry began to flounder and the cost of living increased. This hardship culminated in strikes, power cuts and the introduction of the three-day working week to conserve electricity and power.

In terms of interior design, the 1970s were a contradictory decade. Design trends ranged from earthy tones (greatly influenced by the back-to-nature movement left over from the hippies and the oil crisis of 1973) to bright, colourful rooms with a futuristic look. Most of all, though, 1970s interiors and design were all about individuality.

DAISY AND AMY'S BEDROOM

Richard came to me looking for help to redesign his daughters' bedroom. In the spirit of 1970s' individuality, his daughters, Daisy and Amy, designed their own mood board for their bedroom, and what they came up with was very reminiscent of the 1970s. As turquoise was a favourite colour, we used this as a starting point to create a funky hang-out.

By the 1970s, the bright colours of the previous decade had morphed into richer shades, such as avocado, turquoise, orange, brown, cream and gold. Our homes were all about tactile textures and bold, geometric patterns.

Using a simple technique, we made the most beautiful felt rug (see page 104), then picked up its strong colour in patchwork throws and cushions made from bright period fabric. We also covered a pinboard in toning floral fabric (see page 180 to make your own).

Amy and Daisy love butterflies and wanted them to be a key feature, so we found a beautiful butterfly print wallpaper and used it to create a feature wall. On another wall we used other vintage wallpapers to create a tree mural that also cleverly incorporated shelves for displaying knick-knacks (see page 86).

Furniture in the 1970s tended to be chunkier than previously. Dark woods, such as teak, were very popular, but pine was also widely used, often combined with chrome, glass, tubular steel and plastic for a futuristic feel. If you prefer the earthy 1970s' look, try wicker, rattan or bamboo furniture instead.

Richard found a fantastic old beside cabinet, which he painted to match the colour scheme. Above this he hung a gorgeous mirror that he bought at Newbury Market. Finally, a felt garland made in mixed colours (see page 174) brought the room's many textures and colours together.

Opposite: *Daisy and Amy's fabulous funky bedroom has loads of fun and colourful ideas from the 1970s.*

CREATE YOUR OWN LOOK BOOK

We call it a look book, but it can be a pinboard, a shelf, a cupboard or a box. Whatever it's called, it is a collection of bits and pieces that will potentially inform and inspire all the decisions you make about how to decorate your home.

Each family who participated in the TV series took inspiration from things they loved, and that should be the basis of your scheme too. Pick out favourite things from your home, such as heirlooms, fabrics, old photographs or random knick-knacks. Janine and Shaun had a beautiful green tea set, for example, and that colour played an important part in their playroom scheme. Amber and Colin, on the other hand, had a fantastic red rug, so red became the accent colour in their living room. Anything goes as long as you love it.

Once you've chosen your inspirational items, start adding other inspiring pieces as you come across them. Collect colour swatches and paint charts; cut pictures from magazines; look in books and online. Keep your eyes open because inspiration can come from anywhere at any time.

By bringing everything together in your look book, you'll really get a feel for what you want your room to look like. Once you've built your look book, you'll have a design vision for your room.

Opposite: *The look book for Amber and Colin's living room included patterns and colour swatches typical of the 1960s.*

COLIN → AMBER

BABY

BETTIE

60s

FREELIFE MÉRIDA
FOREST
76500 g/m² 100

140

215

LIVING ROOM

of Men in Californi—
s Approval

he A. E. F. organization,
Service, were explained
on of March 6 by Chaplain
ee in the course of a con-
luncheon in Souilly at
General Kuhn, the division
was guest of honor Chap-
nting various units in the
th, headed by Chaplain
nedict, senior chaplain of
were present.

ee, who is one of the lead-
mrades in Service move-
rom Paris for the confer-
inted out that the aims of
organization are to create
ype of morale; to develop
of citizenship and to bind
lasting comradeship, all
th military and auxiliary.
he army and navy.

g of the movement, Gen-
d the idea was commend-
d he believed the organi-
meet with the approval
and men of the Seventy
sented to them properly.
k up interest in the Com-
vice soon will visit the

D MEETING

r Members in
Ninth Division
scussed

ormal gathering of
e Seventy Ninth was
umont-sur-Aire last
under the auspices
e order in the
More than 100
ent, representing
different states.
per with an ela-
Afterward, there
est and interest in a
get-together of all
e Seventy Ninth was
speakers.

M. G. BN. LOSES

n Train Takes Fast
l Game at Souilly

Ammunition Train de-
h Machine Gun Battalion
e of basketball at Souilly
a score of 31 to 18. The
ers put up a game fight,
considerably outweighed
nition Train.
e most brilliant playing
a done by Lieut. Austin,
r the machine gunners,
ver the court, his floor
shooting being of first
of the same team, also
curate shooting at the

---

drink t
well-tra
who fo
the An
all ov
ty-nin

We
ninth
more
the A
ninth as a whole is very od. But
to give one regiment the credit of a
whole division's fighting is absolutely absurd.

If you come down to fine points
and find out what division made the
last and most effective drive of the
four years of the war you will find
the Seventy-ninth was not present,
but were in some rest camp, where
you forget war
WAGONER WM. H. GRAY,
Headquarters Co., 112th M. G. B.,
Twenty-ninth Division, A. E. F.
France, Nov. 28.

HOTELS TO TAKE
MORE OFFICERS

Low Rates to Commissioned
Personn
Lea

Additional a
hotels for officer
leave in Paris
by the Officers'
city. All rooms
The opening up
officers is the
between the Le
French Ministry
Paris hotels wi
1,000 officers.

Among the Pa
in the agreemen
Deux-Monde C
Orsay, Continent
pole. The agreem
lieve the difficulty many officers find
in getting stopping places in Paris.
The Hotel du Louvre, which is con-
trolled by a Military Board of Directors
is filled to capacity each day.
Officers arriving in Paris can use
busses marked "American Officers,
Bus" in getting to the Hotel du Louvre
or, if that hostlery be filled, in going
to the Officers' Leave Bureau, which
is in No. 4 Avenue Gabriel, at the
Place de la Concorde. Applications for
accommodations in the above hotel-
should be made at the Leave Bureau
before six o'clock P. M.

PENTATHLON SCHEDULED

Divisional Championship Will
Be Decided by May 1

Orders have been issued for the pen-
tathlon, so that the competition for the
divisional championship will be completed by May 1. Regimental championships will be concluded by April 5.
Brigade championships by April 19.

---

be held at Le Mans in May. The
division will also enter men in the individual competition in rifle and pistol
shooting.

One platoon of fifty eight men from
each division will be entered, in the
musketry event. This will not be a
picked platoon, but will be selected
whole from one of the infantry companies. The G. H. Q. order authorizing
the shoot strictly prohibits strengthen-
ing a good platoon by transferring poor
shots out of it and good shots into it.
If the platoon is below strength, it may
be filled up by transferring men from
the particular company to which it be-
longs into it; but no man not in the
company may be drawn on.

This arrangement promises to make
for strong rivalry between different
companies to represent the division.
There is naturally less interest in a
picked team than in a team drawn
whole from one unit.

One man will be selected b

VINTAGE FURNITURE

---

s Energy
Them for Farmin

of Agriculture Cautions
Them, However, Against Plunging
Without Knowing the Game

Discussing the practicability of making arrangements whereby A. E. F.
men could go to farming after they are
discharged from the service, Carl
Vrooman, who visited the division last
week, expressed a firm conviction that
the energy and training of the American
soldiers would make them splendid
farmers.

"The whole spirit of the American
Army," said Mr. Vrooman, "is that a
difficulty exists only to be overcome.
The American soldiers are energetic.
Their life in the army teaches them an
active, outdoors existance, and many of
them will dread to go back to indoor
occupations after the life in the open
they have led in the army.

Country Needs Farmers

"There are various plans being con-
sidered to encourage the American
soldier to take up farming after he gets
out of the army. If he will be careful
of what he is doing, the opportunities

The Educat
Seventy Ninth Division, organi
in compliance with G.O. 30, G. H.
will start next week. Men who
going to take courses at the cen
have been ordered to report
Ambulance-de-Ravigny, Saturd

Eleven courses have been p
vided at the school, five of wh
are vocational, the remaining six
ing in line of general educati
The vocational subjects are: M
chanical Drawing, Salesmansh
Surveying, Cooking and Baki
The general education subjects a
Algebra, Trigonometry, Economi
American and English Literatu
Advanced French, and Advanc
History.

In addition to these subje
Carpentry, Road Construction, a
Automobile Repairing will be tau
away from the center at Ville
sur-Meuse, Recourt, and Souil
respectively.

Salesmanship proved the m
popular of the courses offer
One hundred and twenty will ta
this course. The next most popu
was Mechanical Drawing. In
742 men will received instructi

---

that will be offered will undoubtedly
a splendid thing for him, and for
country; for the country needs
farmers—many more than it has.

"Soldiers who contemplate taking
farming should always remember t
farming is a business one has to
thoroughly familiar with before
can make money out of it. If a sold
does not know much about
farm, he had better plan to learn
great deal about it before buying la
and getting into business for hims
If possible he should go to an agric
tural college, and supplement his cou
there by working on a farm and lea
ing the practical end of it. If he
unable to attend a college, he sho
put in a year or more working fo
successful farmer. I say 'succes
farmer;' it is highly important that
beginner learn farming methods fro
man who has made them pay—

(Continued on Page 4)

Whether you are after original period furniture or second-hand bargains to create your vintage look, this chapter will help you to start seeing the potential. There is always something out there that's right for you. Just follow my advice about planning, searching and selection, and you can find fantastic pieces of furniture for your home. And if they need a bit of TLC, check out my techniques for restoring and looking after furniture so it will last and last and give a wonderful vintage look to your home.

WHAT DO YOU NEED?

Furniture is the staple of every room, but what do you really need? Here are my rules on what to buy.

Rule 1: Start with the basics, thinking about them as the building blocks of your room. In the living room somewhere to sit is a must, so begin with a sofa and/or armchairs. The kitchen is all about cooking and eating, so think about a table and chairs. Bedrooms are for sleeping, so it's comfy beds all the way. With these basics you have a functioning room. Everything else can follow in time. The important point with essentials is to pick pieces you love because you will have to live with them every single day, and probably for a long time.

Rule 2: Don't cram your room with too much furniture. Start with the bare minimum and add other pieces over time. A bit of breathing space between purchases is sometimes a good thing. When buying, look for furniture that might be able to serve a dual purpose. For example, I always think about storage potential when I'm buying any item of furniture because if a key piece can provide storage too, it's a winner in my book.

Rule 3: Buy the best quality you can afford. Flatpack furniture will come and go, often very quickly, but classic, well-made furniture will stand the test of time. Up and down the country in auction houses, markets and thousands of second-hand shops, there is beautiful, high-quality furniture for sale, and it will enhance your home in ways that flatpack can never match. Invest in the good stuff whenever you can.

Rule 4: Think practically. The furniture you choose should work for you and the way you live your life. It shouldn't be a hassle or a maintenance nightmare.

If, for example, you have a busy family life, glass tables and white sofas might not be the best choices if you want to be able to relax. Pick your furniture to make you happy.

Using these rules and carefully considering your furniture choices before you buy will pay dividends in your home, I promise.

CHOOSING FURNITURE

It might sound obvious, but when looking for furniture, always check that the pieces you fall for will fit in your room. And I don't mean style-wise, although of course that is important. You don't want to get a new purchase home and find that you can't even get it through the door. If you've followed my 10 Steps to Planning a Room on page 25, you will have a plan of your room on graph paper with all your key information and options mapped out. These initial ideas don't have to be regarded as set in stone, but they can really help focus your mind when you are buying.

Now the fun starts – the shopping! When you're selecting furniture, it can be difficult to judge the size and how it will fit into your home, so keep your tape measure and room plan to hand. A large table in a warehouse with high ceilings might look in proportion, but in a small room with low ceilings it will look enormous. Remember too that vintage pieces from different eras come in different sizes than the furniture we have today. For example, sofas made in the 1930s and 1940s had bulky frames to bear the weight of heavy stuffing and fabrics, whereas those from the 1950s started to be made with lighter weight materials, meaning that the frames could be more delicate. It's all about scale, so check against your plan and you'll soon see if a particular item would work for you. I know it's all too easy to get carried away when you see something you love.

One last point: remember that sometimes, despite all your careful lists and plans, instinct will dictate what is right for you. It's like house hunting. Often the people I meet have a huge list of requirements and I show them lots of properties that tick all the boxes, but in the end it's the slightly off-brief, wild card property that they end up buying. Heart and head don't always agree, and in this case I generally advise people to trust their instincts. With interiors, you can always move furniture from room to room and play around with it to make it work.

COMBINING VINTAGE FURNITURE

Vintage style is all about mixing and matching to make a room reflect you rather than the past. Your budget may not stretch to having original furniture from your chosen era filling every corner of the room, so selecting one key period piece and combining it with pieces from other eras is a good way to go. If this is your situation, try to choose pieces that have similar shapes, lines or looks to create a sense of unity. For example, the angular look of art deco can work well with the straight lines of wartime utility furniture, while the sleek looks of 1960s' Scandinavian furniture can easily slot into a streamlined 1970s' scheme. In fact, furniture made in similar materials but from different decades can often be successfully married together. Chrome, for example, was popular in both the 1920s and the 1970s, so what's to stop you using pieces from the two decades side by side? The best approach is to go by eye. If you think a particular pairing looks good, just go for it. (For further information about particular styles, see my Vintage Period Guide, page 32.)

Remember that less expensive second-hand furniture can always be customised to pull a look together. The key is seeing its potential. Good ways to evoke a period look in disparate pieces include painting them all the same colour or in toning colours, adding matching vintage handles, or coordinating them with vintage fabric. Janine and Shaun wanted a 1950s-style playroom for their three boys. They already had a dining table and five mismatched chairs that had come from various places and not necessarily from their chosen decade, so together we painted and distressed each chair in bright, 1950s-inspired colours. We then reupholstered each one in matching floral fabric to bring them all together. The table legs were painted in a corresponding colour and the results were fantastic. To create this look yourself, see the projects on pages 66 and 115.

BUYING VINTAGE

A quick glance around any auction house or second-hand shop shows that wooden furniture, such as cabinets, chests and tables, generally tends to hold up well over time. As long as the pieces are solidly constructed and well made, wear and tear can be dealt with in several ways: enjoyed as part of the furniture's history, fixed to make nearly as good as new, or perhaps revitalised with a coat of paint. Upholstered furniture, on the other hand, rarely wears

Opposite: *Old furniture may seem uninspiring at first glance, but maybe it could be repainted or reupholstered to give you the perfect vintage piece for your room.*

well, and if there are any lumps or saggy areas in the stuffing, the whole item could be more expensive to repair than it is actually worth. The key is to check everything very thoroughly before you buy, and here are my tips for doing that.

Try out the item as if you were using it at home. When buying a chair, press on the seat and the back to see if it wobbles and creaks. Lie down on beds. Pull drawers in and out of chests to check they run easily and are aligned properly. Open and close doors on cupboards and wardrobes. They should be flush, and open and close without creaking, lifting or any other problems. Check that the furniture doesn't shake, tremble, sway or even break when you touch it.

Look for strength. In wooden furniture, make sure there aren't any splits or cracks, particularly around knots in the wood. If water has got in, the wood and the knots don't dry at the same rate, and that can lead to problems.

Check that joints are sound and don't have any wobbles. Good-quality wooden furniture is usually held together by dovetail joints or mortise and tenon joints, which simply interlock without screws or glue. To recognise dovetail joints, take a look at the side of an old drawer and you will probably see a series of triangular shapes that interlock like a jigsaw puzzle. Mortise and tenon joints, which consist of a square-cut hole into which a corresponding-shaped peg is slotted, are more likely to be seen on tables or wardrobe doors. Wherever wood is joined, check that the joint is well fitting. If things look bad but you really want the item, it's probably best to pay for a professional repair because a botched DIY job could affect the value of the piece.

Always check for repairs. The most common things to look for are treated cuts, scratches and watermarks on tabletops, and loose joints on chairs. Good repairs should be barely visible and blend in well so that you have to search hard to find them. Bad repairs, on the other hand, are much easier to spot. You might find nails or glue, for example, where a joint has been patched together rather than properly repaired. Of course, repairs can sometimes be part of the patina of a piece, but you should still make sure they have been done properly and won't fall apart when you get the item home.

Give all the surfaces a once-over. If an item is old, you have to accept that there are likely to be scratches, marks and a few bumps and bruises. This can be part of the charm and character, so don't be put off by minor damage.

However, to make sure you are getting a quality item, look for signs of a poor finish, including a rough surface, a very glossy or cloudy surface that hides the grain of the wood, splintered edges or dull spots.

Check for water damage. A milky white ring on a shiny wooden surface indicates that water has penetrated the finish and changed its transparency. (If the ring hasn't been there long, it can sometimes be fixed by gently warming the white patch with a hairdryer, but go carefully as too much heat can do even more damage.) A black ring indicates that water has broken through the finish to the wood underneath, so the damage is more likely to be permanent. Also look out for black marks, raised grain, peeled or lifted veneers, warped wood, slits and waterlogging. The likelihood is that all these problems would need specialist repairs, so buy the piece only if you feel it's really worth it.

Look out for woodworm. The signs are small round holes (a bit like those in a dartboard), fine powdery dust around these holes, and crumbly edges. Don't just check the visible wood – look underneath and behind too. And while you're there, check that nothing else is being patched up or hidden. If you love a piece in dubious condition, my advice is to check with an expert. Woodworm can be treated and isn't always active, so the item might not be a lost cause, but the last thing you want to do is bring insects into your home and infect other items.

When considering upholstered items, check them all over for stains, marks and tears or holes in the fabric. Lift any cushion pads or seats and take a good look (I have heard a few horror stories). Take a sniff. Unpleasant smells, such as smoke, pets and cooking odours, can be difficult (but not impossible) to get rid of. If you're unsure about something or think it doesn't look or smell right, steer clear. If the damage is minimal, remember that torn or worn upholstery can easily be replaced or made good.

Don't forget to check the structure too. When you sit down on a sofa or armchair, the cushion should retain its shape and not curve up around you. Also, you shouldn't be able to feel the frame through the padding, and the back shouldn't feel hollow. I have to admit that I always buy my sofas from auction houses as I love the more traditional designs, but I do make sure they are in good condition and can be reupholstered or will take new loose covers, otherwise they aren't worth it.

Finally, plan your journey home. Sounds obvious, but forget it and you've got one large problem on your hands. A large chest of drawers, for example, won't fit into a Mini, so make sure you've got suitable transport. Vendors in vintage shops, markets or salvage yards might be willing to keep an item for you until you can return to collect it, but that's not likely to happen at a car boot sale.

Similarly, if you are buying online, make sure you can get the item delivered for a reasonable price or can pick it up yourself. Your purchase stops being a bargain if you have to pay extortionate amounts to have it delivered.

VINTAGE TRENDS AND PRICES

Second-hand furniture, like anything else you buy, is subject to fashion. Trends come and go, and the level of demand for particular items will inevitably influence what you have to pay. Just a few years ago dark wood was selling for a fortune at auction houses, but now it's out of vogue and going for a song. That's fine by me because I love it and will buy it regardless of fashion.

Large furniture also doesn't sell too well because most of us just don't have enough space in our homes. If you're lucky enough to have a big house, hefty items such as armoire cupboards, large dining tables and towering dressers could be just what you need, so get out there and bag a bargain.

Of course you should pay a fair price, but I believe everything's up for negotiation, so be prepared to haggle. Damage can be a bargaining tool, but only if you are happy to live with the item as it stands, or if the repair cost won't be more than the piece itself. Remember that if something seems underpriced, there is probably a reason, so be savvy and ask yourself why.

As I keep saying, it's best to buy something because you love it and want to live with it for the foreseeable future. If you always do this, no matter what the trends are, you will never grow tired of what you have.

CLEANING FURNITURE

Always give second-hand furniture a good airing before you let it into the house. Leave it outside for a while, drawers and doors open, although not in direct sunlight, and don't let it get wet. This allows the air to circulate and will get rid of any lurking moths as they absolutely hate the sun.

I always line drawers and wardrobes with scented lining paper. If you don't have any, brown paper will do the job, and you can add a drop of lemon oil or orange oil on a regular basis to get rid of stubborn smells.

Remember that wood, especially old wood, can be damaged by water, so don't rush in with the rubber gloves on, even if you are tempted. Instead, start with a soft paintbrush to get rid of dust and dirt. After that, apply polish (preferably natural beeswax) with a soft cloth and rub it gently over the whole piece to give a rich and protective shine. Silicone-based polishes, like those found in supermarkets, may give an instant shine, but they don't protect the wood in the long term.

If you've bought an upholstered item, a good airing is a must before you clean it. If you can't remove the fabric, an off-the-shelf upholstery cleaner can be used in situ (always do a test on a hidden area first), or a steam cleaner will also give good results. If you don't want to do this yourself, there are companies who will come to your house and do it for you.

If it's just spot stains you want to remove from upholstery, try a mild solution of washing-up liquid or laundry detergent (again, always test a hidden area first). For stubborn stains, apply neat white vinegar and leave on the stain for several minutes. After that, wash in a mild soap solution, then rinse with clean water. Dry as quickly as possible.

For more on how to clean and care for fabrics, see page 95.

REINVENTING FURNITURE

Buying old furniture sometimes requires a leap of the imagination to see the potential of an item rather than what it is now. As long as it's not a rare antique or a valuable family heirloom, getting your sleeves rolled up and putting your stamp on a piece to make it work in your vintage scheme is a fantastic experience. Creating something with your very own hands can't be underestimated. Here are some ideas for how to do it.

Painting is a really great way of revitalising furniture and it needn't be expensive. Almost any type of wooden furniture can be painted (see page 66).

Colour inside as well as out. It's great when you open a wardrobe door and a splash of internal colour meets your eye. Why not try clashing colours inside and out to make a statement, or pretty things up by matching or toning?

Paper rather than paint. If you want a different kind of statement, use wallpaper on the inside of furniture. We did this to great effect on some bedside cabinets made from old drawers (see page 83). Vintage wallpaper also looks great in panels, such as on wardrobe doors. Just cut it to size and glue in place for a flash of colour.

Découpage is an amazing technique that involves glueing decorative paper onto surfaces. It will totally transform any piece of furniture and give it spades of individuality. Simply paint your piece of furniture as explained on page 66. When thoroughly dry, apply PVA glue to a smallish area at a time and apply your chosen paper (old photographs printed onto thin paper give a real vintage feel). Work methodically over the whole piece, brushing glue over the paper just stuck down and overlapping it with the next piece of glued paper. Smooth out any air bubbles with a paintbrush as you go. Once the furniture is dry, paint with varnish to seal.

Changing the handles on a chest of drawers can completely transform it. Vintage handles, which can be picked up at markets and in antique and vintage shops, are easy to fit and can have real impact. They don't even have to match; in fact, I think it looks better if they don't. Start picking up handles when you're out second-hand shopping – you'll be amazed where you find them. Eleanor and Nick found great 1930s' handles in a salvage yard, while Amber and Colin struck lucky at a market, where they found gorgeous blue ones that went perfectly with their 1960s' colour scheme. In both cases, the handles were a real wow factor in their rooms. For a finishing touch, hanging tassels over handles looks fun and adds another layer of personality (see page 139 for more finishing touches).

Mirror glass makes a great new surface for a tabletop. Ask your local glazier to cut a sheet to the correct size, then attach it to the table with sticky pads or mirror adhesive. (Don't be tempted to use ordinary strong glue because it will eventually eat its way through the mirror.)

Decorative veneers come in a huge range of colours and designs, and can easily be applied to furniture to make it uniquely your own.

Silk-screen printing on furniture is another fantastic technique for adding beautiful pattern and colour (see the project on page 80).

Opposite: *Having used the distressing technique so successfully on their playroom chairs, Shaun and Janine used it again to great effect on a 1950s' dressing table.*

KIRSTIE'S GUIDE TO DIY

Doing up, reinventing and rejuvenating furniture is incredibly satisfying, but it does require a few DIY skills. Please don't let that put you off. Like any other skill, such as knitting or crochet, DIY is a craft that you can conquer with a bit of practice, but where to begin?

In my opinion, you should start by acquiring a basic toolkit, but it should contain the best tools you can afford. Before you splash out on brand new, try buying second-hand: you'll be amazed what people sell or give away. As for the bigger stuff, borrowing it will only cost you the price of a box of chocolates or a bottle of wine to say thank you, so ask around friends and neighbours if you need something specialist.

Another thing to plunder is people's knowledge. Next time you have a handyman in to fix something, watch what he is doing, ask questions and you might pick up a thing or two.

STARTER TOOLKIT

Tool box (This doesn't have to be anything fancy. Pick something that keeps everything together in the one place. A plastic box with lots of compartments or a bag with several pockets will do the job fine. If it doesn't have somewhere separate to keep nails, screws and all the other small bits that you accumulate, save clear plastic tubs used for dips and put your bits in them.)

Tape measure

Claw hammer

Insulated pliers

Set of screwdrivers

Junior hacksaw

Stanley knife

Spirit level

Adjustable spanner

Other items to consider:

Set of paintbrushes in a variety of sizes

Paint roller and tray

Sandpaper

Nails and screws in a variety of sizes (although these can be bought as and when required)

Two-speed electric drill plus a range of drill bits

A toolkit is an ever-changing collection that can be added to as the need arises. In a surprisingly short time, you'll always have the right tool on hand, whatever the job.

Opposite: *Examples of screen-printed furniture. As you can see, screen-printing is a great way to enliven otherwise plain wooden items.*

*Distressed CHAIR *

Doing up old, second-hand furniture is a must to achieve the vintage look in your home, whatever era you are going for. One of the best ways to completely transform an old piece is by painting and distressing it. Simon Bell, who owns a second-hand furniture shop in west London, specialises in this technique, and he shared his secrets with me when I did up a chair at my Vintage Café. It really is an easy and straightforward technique, and has amazing results. What was a dull old chair became a bright and wonderful piece of furniture.

To make it work effectively with your chosen vintage era, do your research and choose a colour that was typical of the time, or take inspiration from a vintage fabric.

You will need

Dustsheets or newspaper, as required

Chair of your choice (the seat should be removed if it's a drop-in type)

Apron or overalls

Safety goggles

Rubber gloves

Sugar soap (fantastic for cutting through grease and grime)

Measuring jug (optional)

Bucket

Cloth

Medium sandpaper

Large soft brush and/or duster

2 colours of one-coat matt emulsion: brilliant white for an undercoat, and your chosen colour for a top coat

3 paintbrushes, 7.5–10 cm wide (1 for each colour and the varnish)

1 paintbrush, 1–2 cm wide, for painting any details (optional)

Putty knife

Coarse fabric-backed sandpaper

Flexible sanding tool (optional)

Decorator's clear satin varnish

HEALTH AND SAFETY NOTE
• Wear protective goggles, gloves and old clothes • Cover nearby surfaces throughout the process. • Follow the manufacturer's instructions when using sugar soap as it can dry the skin and cause irritation to the eyes and lungs.

5

6

1. Cover your working area with dustsheets or newspaper, then place your chair in the centre. If you stand it on a table, as we did, it saves you having to bend or kneel.

2. Wearing protective clothing, goggles and rubber gloves, prepare the sugar soap according to the manufacturer's instructions. Dip your cloth in the solution, then use it to wash down the chair. Rinse off with clean warm water, then allow the chair to dry.

3. Lightly sand the chair with medium sandpaper. Don't be tempted to skip this stage: it's important as the roughened surface gives the paint better 'grip'. When you've finished, brush the chair to get rid of any dust.

4. Apply a thick coat of the white emulsion using a wide brush. Take care – you don't want any drips. Inspect your work carefully, then go around touching up any parts you've missed (you might want to use a narrow brush to get right into any decorative details on the wood). Leave to dry.

5. Use a second wide brush to paint your chosen colour on top of the white. Again, try to avoid drips, then go around touching up your work, using a narrow brush for any details if you wish. Leave to dry, ideally for no more than a day, or the paint will be too hard to distress easily in the next step.

6. To achieve the distressed look, scrape a putty knife along the edges and corners of the chair to remove some of the paint. The idea is to target the areas that would naturally get worn. Now take some coarse sandpaper, wrapped around a flexible sanding tool if you like, and sand off more paint on the scraped areas.

7. Get rid of the dust by using a soft brush or duster, then apply two coats of varnish to the chair, allowing it to dry between coats. Slot the seat back into the finished chair to dry between coats.

Wooden TREASURE CHEST

Creating your very own handmade, vintage-inspired items for the home doesn't have to be restricted to just the smaller finishing touches. Anselm Fraser, from the Chippendale International School of Furniture, gave Shaun and Janine a lesson in how to make a wooden chest, and they ended up making it in three different sizes – one for each of their sons. To tie in with their 1950s' theme, they painted the chests white and stencilled a boy's name on the front in suitable vintage lettering. Apart from being fantastic for storage, the chests are unique handmade heirlooms that the boys can treasure forever.

If you fancy trying your hand at furniture making, do an online search to find classes near you. It is a skill really worth investing in as the end result is beautiful and the process extremely satisfying. Here are Anselm's instructions.

CHOOSING YOUR MATERIALS

To make your very own wooden treasure chest, it's best to use new wood (Shaun and Janine used pine) and give it a vintage twist with painted decoration. However, reclaimed wood can be used if you prefer, but do ensure it hasn't been varnished before or it won't glue together well.

CUTTING THE WOOD

The measurements given below are for the largest of the three wooden chests, but can be scaled to whatever size you like on graph paper. You will need 12 pieces of 18 mm pine cut as follows:

Front and back: 920 x 520 mm each

2 sides: 550 x 520 mm each

Lid, top: 930 x 580 mm

Lid, front lip: 970* x 40 mm

Lid, side lips: 660* x 40 mm each

Base: 920 x 556 mm

Front skirting: 990* x 120 mm

2 side skirtings: 610* x 120 mm each

Name plate: 400 x 85 mm

*These measurements are slightly overlength so they can be cut exactly to size on the job.

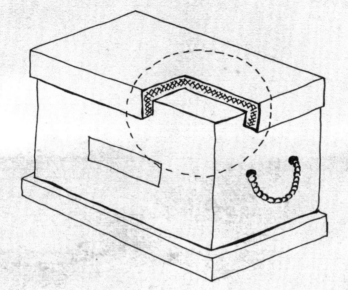

A timber merchant will cut the timber to size for you. If you prefer to do it yourself, carefully measure and mark out each piece, writing its position (front, side, etc.) on it too. Clamp the wood to a bench with the excess sticking out and saw along your pencil marks. The excess will fall to the floor.

NOTE: The wood can be painted before or after the box is put together – the choice is yours.

DRILLING THE FIXING HOLES

Shaun and Janine used stepped wooden pegs (Miller Dowel System) to put their box together because it was more in keeping for a vintage style, but this requires a stepped drill bit, so you might need to ask a carpenter for help. Mark out where the fixing holes will be drilled. The number of holes doesn't matter, as long as they are evenly spaced, so measure them out carefully.

JOINING THE PIECES TOGETHER

With the holes now drilled, the next step is to paint PVA wood glue onto the wooden pegs and tap them in with a hammer. The order in which the pieces are joined together is as follows:

1. Carcass – attach one long side to one short side; do the same with the other two sides, then join these two L-shaped pieces together.
2. Base – screw this to the carcass.
3. Skirting – peg together, then screw in place around the base at the front and sides.
4. Lid and name plate – see below.

ATTACHING THE LID

Cheap 7.5 cm hinges are fine for fixing the lid to the box, but you can give them a vintage look by sanding them and painting them with blackboard paint. When they're dry, mark out their fixing holes on the lid and the back of the box. Drill the holes, screw the hinges to the box, then attach them to the lid. Check that the lid fits properly and adjust if necessary.

If you want to stop the lid from falling backwards, you can do as Shaun and Janine did, and attach chains inside the box with washers and screws. Mark out the fixing holes on the lid and sides and drill the screws in directly to hold the washers in place. (In this instance, you do not need to pre-drill the fixing holes.)

MAKING HANDLES

For a lovely extra touch, drill two holes in each side of the box and thread with rope, knotting it on the inside to make handles.

ADDING THE NAME PLATE

Stencil a name on the name plate. (To make your own stencil, see the invitation project on page 198.) Glue the name plate to the front of the box and voilà! One lovely treasure chest.

Rejuvenated OTTOMAN

If you want to rejuvenate a piece of upholstered furniture quickly and easily, this is the project for you. It truly is a cheat's guide to upholstery.

You will need

Ottoman or similar piece of furniture that needs new upholstery

Tape measure

Pen

Foam

Scissors

Fabric

Double-sided sticky tape

Staple gun (take care to use it in an open area with no pets or children around)

1. Remove any old coverings from the ottoman, and discard the padding too if it's tatty. Measure the top of the ottoman. Cut a piece of foam that's 5 mm bigger all round, then cut a piece of fabric, adding 10 cm all round. Using a few pieces of double-sided sticky tape, stick the foam to the top of the ottoman.

2. Place the fabric over the foam, centring it as necessary, then hold the material and pull the front edge to the underside of the lid, tucking it behind the lip inside the box. Staple the fabric behind the lip at the centre front, then do the same at the centre back and the centre of each side. (It's important not to put the staples along the top edge of the box.) Get someone to help if you can – one person to stretch and hold the fabric while the other staples.

3. At the corners, make neat tucks in the fabric (like hospital corners on a bed) and staple as before.

4. With the lid closed, draw a V-shape on the fabric about 5 mm below each hinge: the top of the V should be as wide as the hinge, and the point of it should meet the edge of the fabric. Cut along each V and tuck the resulting triangles of fabric under the main fabric covering the foam.

5. Open the lid of the ottoman again and continue stapling from the inside whilst pulling the fabric taut to hold it securely in place.

Bedside CABINETS

Upcycling is a huge part of making the vintage home, and I love nothing more than finding new ways of using old things. When I helped make over Janine and Shaun's bedroom, they needed new bedside tables, but couldn't find anything they liked within their budget. Cue a trip to a salvage yard to find a pair of old wooden filing cabinet drawers that cost a fiver each, and that we transformed by lining the inside with wallpaper. Cheap, simple and really effective – it's easy when you know how, so give it a go.

You will need

Old wooden drawers or crates

Sandpaper

Tape measure

Pencil and paper

Wallpaper

Scissors

Wallpaper paste

MDF, same size as back of drawer

Wood glue

Spirit level

Drill with appropriate drill bits

Wall plugs and corresponding screws

Screwdriver

1. Check over the drawers and sand off any rough edges. Measure the inside surfaces where you want the wallpaper to go. Make a note of the measurements, then cut a piece of wallpaper to fit. We covered only the top, bottom and sides with wallpaper, but you could also do the back if you wish, but only once the cabinet is hung. Paste the wallpaper to the inside and leave to dry.

2. Reinforce the back of each cabinet by attaching a piece of MDF with wood glue. When dry, drill two holes in the back of the cabinet, approximately 5 cm from the top and sides. Mark the wall in pencil where you want the cabinets to go, checking for straightness with a spirit level. Drill holes in the wall and insert wall plugs. Screw the cabinets to the wall.

Memory BOX

Seeing the potential of second-hand furniture takes practice, but you can have so much fun along the way. And there's no better justification for making regular trips to second-hand shops, markets, salvage yards and auctions – they're the only way to develop a good eye. It's also worth looking at things you already own and seeing if they can be put to better or different use. You might give yourself a nice surprise.

Janine and Shaun already had a lovely distressed-looking display cabinet, but it really wasn't being used to best effect, so I decided to show them how to make it much more special and personal by turning it into a memory box. You can easily do this too by following the steps below.

You will need

Small cabinet with shelves   Pins

Personal items and photographs   Polishing cloth

Blu-Tack

I. Decide whether you like your cabinet the way it is. Would you prefer to paint and distress it? If so, see page 66 for a guide to that technique. Once your cabinet is ready, attach it to the wall or place on a shelf.

2. Now make a selection of favourite personal items. If you don't have anything that inspires you, shop around for old things, such as sepia photographs, vintage books, postcards, small bottles, jewellery, pill-boxes and anything else that takes your fancy. It's a good idea to theme your items, and this can be done by selecting similar colours or patterns, or things from the same era (see pages 144–7 for more about this).

3. Give all your chosen items a good polish and begin to create your display. Start by placing photographs, postcards and larger items towards the back of the shelves, propping them up, or fixing with Blu-tack or pins as necessary. Gradually work towards the front of the cabinet, arranging the smaller items so that they can be clearly seen. As our photo shows, the result is both interesting and attractive – a source of pleasure every time you glance its way.

SCREEN-PRINTED *Sideboard*

Picking up second-hand furniture is a really great way to furnish your home. Not only do you get something unique, but you also have something ripe for renovation and ready for you to put your personal stamp on.

Amber and Colin picked up a 1960s' sideboard for a steal online, and whilst there was nothing much wrong with it, they wanted to give it a really funky edge. Designer Zoe Murphy specialises in screen-printing furniture in a retro style, so she was just the person to come along to my Vintage Café and give us all a lesson. She worked with Amber and Colin to design a stencil that suited their 1960s' theme, and their sideboard went from being a utilitarian piece of furniture to a swinging vintage focal point for their living room.

Screen-printing is a really easy technique, and once you've had a bit of practice, it becomes quite addictive. The screen required has a wooden or metal frame, and, depending on size, can be bought ready-made or in kit form from specialist suppliers, craft shops or online. The trickiest part of the process is making the design that becomes the stencil on the screen, but even that's pretty straightforward – and, of course, it can be used over and over again. Look online for your local friendly screen-printing studio and ask them to give you a hand. Studios often run courses where you can learn the whole screen-printing process.

You will need

Piece of furniture with flat surfaces

Tape measure

Silk screen, of suitable size for your furniture and design

Pencil and paper

3 paintbrushes: 1 for the light-sensitive emulsion, 1 for the paint, 1 for the varnish

Light-sensitive emulsion

Black marker pen with thickish nib

Sheet of acetate

Light box

Fine sandpaper

Damp cloth

Masking tape

Water-based paint, emulsion or acrylic

Squeegee, to fit inside your silk screen (an old credit card can be used if your screen is very small)

Decorator's varnish, matt or gloss, as you prefer

1. Examine your piece of furniture and decide what area of it you want to screen-print. Once you've decided and measured the area, you can buy a silk screen of the right size.

2. Sketch your design on paper, making sure it will fit on your furniture and within the silk screen.

3. Brush the silk in the frame on both sides with light-sensitive emulsion and leave it to dry for 30 minutes.

4. Meanwhile, using a thick black pen, copy your design neatly onto a sheet of acetate that will fit inside your screen. Lay the acetate design on a light box, place the screen on top, flat side down, then blast with light for around 20 seconds. Rinse the frame under running water, and you will see that the light has not penetrated the black areas of the design, so the silk has now become a stencil.

5. Using fine sandpaper, quickly and lightly sand the furniture surface to be screen-printed so that the sanding can barely be seen. The idea is to create a 'key' for the paint to stick to. Wipe with a damp cloth to make it clean and dust-free, then leave to dry.

6. Position your furniture so that the surface you want to print on is perfectly horizontal. You might have to turn it on its side to do this. If you want to print onto drawers or doors, you need to remove them and take off any handles.

7. Using masking tape, mark out where you want the edge of the screen-print to be. This ensures that the printing won't be done on the wrong area. Top tip: if your surface has a veneer or special coating on it, stick the masking tape to your clothes or a piece of scrap wood before you put it onto the furniture; that way it will lose some of its stickiness, and there'll be less risk of it lifting off the surface and leaving a mark.

8. If you wish, a water-based background colour can be painted onto the masked area before it's screen-printed. If you decide to do this, leave plenty of time for it to dry before you start the printing process.

9. Position the screen on the masked-out area and pour some paint inside it along one end.

10. Using a squeegee, pull the paint towards you. This might need to be done more than once if your squeegee is narrower than the screen.

11. Carefully remove the screen, lifting it up from one side so as not to smudge the paint. Leave the furniture to dry.

12. Repeat steps 9, 10 and 11 on other parts of the furniture as often as you wish. When you have finished, thoroughly wash the silk screen to remove all the paint.

13. Paint the printed area with two coats of varnish to seal it, allowing it to dry between each coat.

Tree
MURAL WITH SHELVES

This unique mural, which cleverly incorporates shelves, really is a work of art. Created by Junior Phipps, a 3-D designer who has produced sets for stages all over the world, it uses vintage-inspired wallpaper for the tree, leaves and butterflies, and reclaimed wood for the front of the shelves, which are cleverly shaped to blend in with the branches. I think it's absolutely brilliant, and so did Richard's daughters Daisy and Amy, who couldn't wait to use it.

To create something similar but give it your very own look, you could use vintage wallpaper, old books or vintage posters. With a bit of imagination, even the humble shelf can be given a vintage twist and become a fantastic focal point.

Our shelves were made in two lengths: 78 cm and 50 cm, and both were 22 cm deep, but you can make them any size you like, depending on how much space you have.

You will need

Tape measure

Paper and pencil

Masking tape

Vintage wallpapers

Scissors or scalpel

Sewing machine

Thread

Blu-tack

Wallpaper paste and brush

1.5 metres of 22 x 2.5 cm plywood, for the shelves

Saw

1.5 metres of 5 x 2.5 cm plywood, for battens (optional)

1.5 metres of 13 x 2.5 cm wood, preferably reclaimed, for the shelf fascias

G-clamps

Jigsaw

Electric drill

Screws (ours were 7 mm)

Screwdriver

Fine sandpaper

Wood filler

Screw-in hooks (optional)

Wall plugs, to match your screw size

Paint or varnish (optional)

2a

2b

2c

1. Measure the area in which you want to install the mural, then sketch out your design, trying to keep things in proportion. (Working on graph paper will make this easier.) Our mural had two shelves, but you can incorporate as many as you like.

2. Using masking tape, stick a sheet of suitable wallpaper for the tree trunk and branches to the wall, blank side facing you. Draw the trunk and branches onto it, then take the paper down and cut around the shapes. On the back of different wallpapers, draw your leaves, flowers and butterflies, then cut these out too (photos 2a, 2b). Sew a butterfly to a flower or leaf, stitching along its centre, then fold the wings together to make them stick out. You can also stitch some of the leaves into clusters (photo 2c).

3. Using Blu-tack, stick the wallpaper trunk to the wall, then attach the branches, leaves, flowers and butterflies in the same way. When you are happy with the arrangement, stick each piece in place with wallpaper paste.

4. Cut the plywood for the shelves to the required length, then cut the battens to the same length. Cut the ends of the battens at a slight angle (see photo 6).

5. Now cut the pieces for the branch-shaped fascias from the reclaimed wood. They should be the same length as the shelves.

6. Mark out your branch design in pencil on the fascia pieces. Stand a shelf along the centre of each fascia and draw along both sides of it. This will give you a rough idea of where you will later screw the two pieces together. Clamp a fascia to your workbench using G-clamps, and use a jigsaw to cut around the design.

7. Mark out the location of all your fixing holes on the shelf in pencil. Depending on the size of your shelf, you need 3–4 holes about 30 cm apart along each side and at the corresponding places on the battens and fascias. Pre-drill all these holes, using a drill bit that corresponds to the size of your screws. Align the shelf to the batten and screw them together. Now screw the branch fascia to the front edge of the shelf, using G-clamps to hold things firmly in place while you do so.

8. All three pieces of wood are now fixed together. Depending on the condition of the wood, you might like to sand the edges to get rid of any splinters. When that is done, cover any screw heads with wood filler and sand smooth.

9. If you want to add screw-in hooks to the underside of the shelves for more storage, do so at this stage.

10. Mark the position of the shelf on the wall and where its fixing holes should be. Using a masonry drill bit (ours was 7 mm, a good size for a heavy shelf), drill fixing holes in the wall. Insert wall plugs into the drilled holes, then screw the battened side of the shelf to the wall.

11. Paint or varnish the shelves as you wish, or leave them as they are if you have used lovely reclaimed wood.

* SOFT *
FURNISHINGS

There is a glorious variety of fabrics and textiles available to enhance and embellish our homes. They are known collectively as soft furnishings, an old-fashioned term that does little to evoke the wealth of colour and comfort they can bring to our surroundings with a little help from our own imagination.

The rugs, hangings, linens, quilts, cushions, throws and upholstery that are so much a part of life today were originally luxuries, found only in the grandest of homes when they were first used in Britain during the seventeenth century. Their purpose, though, was very similar – to create a warm, welcoming and relaxing haven. The difference now is that there are soft furnishings to suit every budget and in countless different styles. Every home can feel luxurious, loved and lived in.

Apart from making life more comfortable and pleasant, soft furnishings can also make a style statement. They can complement or clash. They can blend in or be a focal point. They can also create a mood. Whether you want glamour, elegance or a cosy cocoon, soft furnishings can help you achieve it.

The exciting thing about using fabrics is their ability to change the look of a room cheaply and almost instantly. So let me show you how to create a nest you want to spend time in and a home you are proud to show off to your friends.

WHERE TO FIND VINTAGE FABRIC

I'm always on the lookout for beautiful second-hand fabrics for my home. I love old linens and vintage florals, and it's easy to pick them up at markets, charity shops, antique warehouses and car boot sales. If you're after vintage fabric from a specific period, you might get lucky in these fertile hunting grounds, but if you are struggling to find what you want, there are specialist shops (many online too) that cater for virtually every taste. The good ones stock a whole wealth of fabrics from many different periods, so if you do want to evoke a certain era in your room, these are the people to make friends with. In my experience, they are always more than willing to have a chat and offer sound advice. They are fellow enthusiasts and experts, so use their knowledge. You might pay more than buying from a junk shop, but if you love a particular fabric and it makes your home that little bit more special, in my eyes it is always worth it.

Do your research first. Discover broadly what type of fabrics will complement your look. For example, big, bright, floral prints will add to a 1950s' theme, while pop art fabric will get the 1960s' party started.

Don't forget to search closer to home too. Before you hit the shops, check out your granny's linen cupboard. You might find a family heirloom, or a wonderful period piece waiting to be resurrected and reused. Could that old evening dress, for example, be turned into cushion covers that might just say '1940s' better than any other fabric you've seen? Keep your mind and eyes wide open and you're likely to find the right fabric for you.

CHOOSING VINTAGE FABRIC

Shopping for vintage takes quite a bit more care than simply buying new. It's essential to check thoroughly what you are buying before you hand over your cash. This is especially true when it comes to vintage fabrics.

Before you buy a piece, make sure you feel the fabric and thoroughly inspect every inch. If it is folded, open it out to get a good look. Does it have any stains or marks? If so, they are almost certainly there to stay, having set over years of scrubbing and washing. Maybe you can accept that they are part of the fabric's history so you can still use it.

Old fabrics may be faded and threadbare. This can be part of their intrinsic charm, but take care you aren't buying something that is about to fall apart. Of course, it is possible to buy vintage fabrics that are in excellent condition, but don't expect perfection. These pieces were probably lightly used and are likely to have survived because they are well made and durable. In fact, what draws me to vintage fabrics again and again is their enduring quality and beauty.

Check for holes and decide if the fabric could be used in a way that conceals them. You might even decide to enjoy the piece as it is, and embrace the history signified by such battle scars. However, do please remember that holes in fabric can be a sign of the dreaded moth. Look carefully and ask the vendor to help. I would recommend staying away from any soft furnishing or fabric that you think might include moths in the price. It is really difficult to rescue a fabric that has moth damage, and if you do take it home and let moths loose, they could cause untold damage to the rest of your soft furnishings. Their favourite place is dark, undisturbed cupboards, so my tip is to use your fabrics or get them out in the open as often as possible for a good airing.

When buying vintage cushions and curtains, feel the seams and check whether the stitching is still firmly in place. If repairs are needed and you are handy with a sewing machine, that's great, but if you're not, you might want to think again (or find someone who can help).

KEY CONSIDERATIONS

When choosing a fabric to make into soft furnishings, it is important to get the right type to ensure successful results. Here are a few key considerations.

Fabric weight and durability. Heavy fabrics, such as ticking, are great for covering sofas and chairs because they are tough and long-lasting. They are less suitable for small items, such as cushions, because they tend to be bulky.

If you find a very lightweight vintage fabric (perhaps silk) that you are desperate to use, backing it with iron-on interfacing gives it more strength.

Washability. Most vintage fabric is likely to have been washed many times before, so any shrinkage will already have happened. If you come across something that looks brand new, it is always a good idea to pre-wash it before making it up to avoid your stitched item shrinking later, getting puckered seams or possibly losing shape. Of course, some fabrics, such as cotton velvet, should always be dry cleaned rather than washed. Take each piece on a case-by-case basis and see the cleaning information below and overleaf.

Fabric width. The wider the fabric, the less sewing required for big items. If you find a fabric that you are desperate to use but it is not wide enough, buy more length to make up for it and accept that there will have to be a seam across the width where you have joined the pieces. And if there's not enough of the fabric to do this, you could join pieces of complementary or even contrasting material to make up to the correct width. The central square of Amber and Colin's patchwork quilt on page 108 does this to great effect.

Pattern repeat. The bigger the pattern, the more fabric you will need to match up the repeat.

In general with vintage fabric, you often have to take what you find, but if you come across a large amount, I would advise you to buy slightly more than you think you will need. It is better to have too much than too little.

CLEANING VINTAGE FABRIC

You'll probably want to clean your vintage fabric to get rid of any unwanted smells or marks, but tread carefully. Some fabrics, and trims such as lace, silk or ribbon, can shrink or distort if washed the wrong way.

Opposite: *Vintage fabric is really easy to find. Even when it's old and faded, it can add so much character to a vintage room.*

You don't want to ruin a beautiful or valuable piece by giving it an over-zealous dunking. If in doubt, seek advice from vintage fabric experts, or consult a professional dry cleaner. Sometimes dry cleaning is the only safe option.

If you decide to try washing it yourself, proceed with caution and treat it as you would any delicate fabric. Check for any washing instructions first. If you find them, it's your lucky day; if you don't, read on. Many well-used, vintage fabrics can be washed, and probably have been countless times over the years. I recommend doing a patch test first to make sure the fabric is colourfast. Lots of old fabrics were created using natural dyes, which may still run even if they have been washed a million times before. Dampen an unseen corner and rub a small amount of soap into it. Leave to dry to see if there is dramatic colour fading or dye seepage. If nothing untoward happens, you can then do a cool and gentle hand wash (rather than a machine wash), using mild wool soap or soap flakes. If you can't face washing a large, heavy item by hand, the safe option is to give your local dry cleaner the job. If you fancy a gamble, use your machine's silk or wool programme on a cool wash.

Never tumble-dry vintage fabric. Ideally, hang it outside (avoiding direct sunlight as this will cause fading) and let it dry in the fresh air.

WHAT TO DO WITH VINTAGE FABRIC

Please use and enjoy your vintage fabrics. It's madness to have bundles of linen sitting in cupboards, never seeing the light of day. I have a huge collection of vintage napkins that I've bought over the years and they get used all the time. I know constant washing will eventually fade them and wear them out, but they're meant to be used, and they give me so much pleasure.

Even when my lovely napkins reach the end of their days, I won't be throwing them out. I'll probably incorporate them into a quilt (see page 108). And if I don't have enough, I can make them into a patchwork cushion. There is always a way of reusing and reinventing fabrics. Old cushion fabric can look great on a lampshade with a few tassels added to glam it up, while old bed linen can make a lovely curtain to cover an open cupboard. I recently interviewed Prince Charles and even he admitted that he has old curtains made into cushions because he can't bear waste. There is no shame in being frugal. If royalty can do it, you can too.

There are so many lovely things that you can do with vintage fabrics. The only limits are the size of your imagination and the amount of fabric you can find. But even small pieces can be used creatively. When I found a beautiful 1940s' fabric, there wasn't enough to make curtains, so I turned it into a blind that I really love.

Here are a few more ideas of what to do with your vintage fabric finds.

Half curtains: Also known as café curtains, these look fantastic in vintage fabric. Use a pretty cotton print or even a lace tablecloth. All you need to do is decide how far up the window you want the curtain to go and measure this height and the width. Select a piece of fabric this size (or join pieces together to make this size), adding a 2.5 cm seam allowance all around, plus 10 cm extra at the top to create a channel for a curtain rod. Hem the bottom and sides, leaving the top till last. Alternatively, hem all four sides, attach rings along the top, then hang from a rod fixed at your chosen height. Simple!

Cushions covers: I adore cushions, and making covers is my favourite way of using vintage fabric. As far as I'm concerned, there is not a chair, bed, sofa, window seat or lonely corner that won't benefit from a cushion covered in gorgeous vintage fabric. Cushions add that personal, comfy touch to a home without a great deal of expense, so if you are new to vintage fabrics, this is a great place to start. I can't recommend it highly enough.

Patchwork: There is no better way of using small pieces of vintage fabrics than making them into patchwork, which can then be used for cushions, quilts, wall hangings, bedspreads and table runners. Page 108 shows you how to make your own patchwork quilt, but what's to stop you creating a patchwork large enough to reupholster a bench or seat? See pages 74 and 115 for how to do this.

Folding chairs: Old director's chairs can get a new lease of life if you replace the torn seat and back with vintage fabric that's strong enough to take a person's weight (canvas, denim or heavyweight cotton are best). Use the old seat covering as a template and fix the new fabric in place with a heavy-duty staple gun.

Knick-knacks: If you have only small scraps of vintage fabric, you could make pincushions, lavender bags, bunting, draft excluders or little stuffed toys (like the novelty cushion I made with Iman and Heather, see page 128). Alternatively, you can display your lovely vintage fabric in a frame or an embroidery hoop and hang it on the wall. You get really lovely multi-window frames nowadays, and these are ideal for displaying a range of vintage fabrics. (See page 147 for my guide on how to hang pictures.)

BASIC SEWING KIT

Each sewing and crafting job will bring new challenges and require new items, so add to the following list of basics as the need arises. A sewing machine is a great investment if you have the money and are committed to using it regularly, but don't rush into buying one until you are sure you will use it.

Tape measure

Pins and a pincushion

Needles (and needle threader if you wish)

Thimble

Threads in various colours (avoid cheap thread as it breaks too easily)

Fabric-marking tool, e.g. water-soluble pen or tailor's chalk (or even a sliver of white, dried-out soap (avoid those containing lots of moisturiser – they are too oily); the great thing is that it won't leave a mark on your fabric after washing or ironing)

Two pairs of scissors (1 pair for fabric, another for paper)

Seam ripper

Selection of hooks and eyes, buttons and poppers

ARRANGING SOFT FURNISHINGS

Once you have sourced the vintage fabric and made all your amazing soft furnishings, what do you do with them? How do you make your room look like the vintage haven you want? Here's my secret – layering.

Creating layers is about combining lots of different soft furnishing elements – window treatments, cushions, rugs and throws – in lots of different textures, colours and patterns. They can be matched or coordinated to bring the room together, or to make a bold, clashing statement that catches the eye. Don't be afraid to mix and match fabrics; it looks more stylish and interesting than a single fabric and makes your room unique.

A good place to start building your room is to look at the large upholstered items, such as sofas and chairs. These provide a really good base on which to start layering your vintage soft furnishings to create the style you want. In the

Opposite: *When you make friends with the owner of your local sewing shop, you not only get great service, but also access to their fund of expert knowledge.*

1970s, for example, the popular look for upholstery was striped fabric in autumn tones of brown and beige. If you go for this, layering the rest of the room with a complementary palette of oranges, blues and earthy greens will bring it all together.

Window treatments are another good starting point. Say you have a 1960s-inspired room with paisley print curtains (all the rage in that decade), your other soft furnishings can pick up colours from the pattern and be made in a variety of textures. What's to stop you having velvet or felt cushions, perhaps with lace, satin or ribbon details? They will all add extra layers of interest and comfort to your room.

Layer patterns too. My advice is to have one dominant pattern plus a complementary pattern in a toning colour. For example, if you have a 1950s-style bold, bright floral on your curtains, you could use a stripe or check to go with it. In this case, I'd advise choosing a narrow stripe or small check because anything bigger alongside your bold floral would be competing for attention.

Cushions, curtains and upholstery are important elements in your room, but don't limit yourself when it comes to soft furnishings. A sofa will look really inviting with a throw placed over the arm or over the back, but do remember that it is meant to be used. I love everything to be neat and tidy in my house, but I want it to be relaxed too. Just as well, because my boys love making dens with my artfully placed throws.

Rugs are a great way of adding texture, colour, pattern and warmth to a room. And if you buy a decent rug, it will be an investment piece that will last and last. Make sure you get your vintage rugs professionally cleaned to make them last even longer.

Overall, when it comes to layering your soft furnishings, instinct is your best guide. If you love the way they sit in a room and you enjoy spending time there, that's all that matters. A loved home is a lived-in home. Go for it!

Opposite: *These fabulous cushions are a cinch to make, and the vintage fabric makes them a stylish addition to any room.*

Punched
FELT RUG

During the 1970s, bright bold patterns and colours were dominant in our homes, and no bedroom at that time was without a bedside rug. While shaggy textures were very fashionable at that time, this project goes for a smoother look, but still captures the mood of the 1970s. Designed by award-winning textile designer Selina Rose, who specialises in working with felt, this project is a stylish way to bring colour, texture and pattern into a room. The basic idea is to draw a design onto a length of felt, then to punch holes along the lines. The technique is simple yet very attractive.

As requested by Richard and his daughters, Daisy and Amy, Selina's design incorporated a beautiful butterfly motif, which worked really well within the girls' 1970s-inspired bedroom. Feel free to recreate it in your chosen colour, or to dream up your own design to make it unique to your vintage home. Placing the finished rug on a neutral or self-coloured carpet will really make the punched design stand out and add the wow factor.

You will need

Pencil and paper (optional)

Length of 100% wool felt 3mm thick (ours measured 100 x 60 cm, but you can make the rug to any size you like)

Sheet of MDF or something similar (to use as a cutting board)

Rotary cutter or craft knife

Steel ruler (if you're cutting straight lines)

Masking tape

Hammer

Steel hole punches (these can be bought cheaply online; we used mainly 5 mm, plus a few larger ones for areas of the wings)

1. If you want to use the butterfly design, photocopy the template below to the size(s) you want it to appear on your rug. Alternatively, sketch out your own design using pencil and paper, and draw small circles on the outline to indicate where the hole punch will be used. Make sure the circles aren't placed too close together, as the idea is to make neat holes that don't overlap. Think about incorporating circles of different sizes into your design to create contrast and interest – for example, large holes for the perimeter and small holes for the inner detail.

2. Place the felt on a large piece of MDF. Using a rotary cutter or craft knife, cut the felt to your chosen shape and size.

3. Place your paper design on the felt and stick it down with masking tape.

4. With your felt still on the MDF, use a hammer and a steel hole punch of the appropriate size to punch holes along the lines of the design, going through both the paper and the felt (photos 4a, 4b). You'll be left with clean cuts, as the punch removes the felt. When you've finished, remove the paper template and the design is revealed in all its glory.

4a

4b

⟞⟞⟞ Appliqué QUILT ⟞⟞⟞⟞⟞

More often than not, vintage fabric is found in small pieces, and it's difficult to know what to make from it so as to show off its particular qualities. Sewing expert Lisa Comfort has come up with this beautiful quilt, which can incorporate both vintage fabrics and 'memory fabrics' (pieces that hold special significance for you) in a design that can be made uniquely personal.

Amber and Colin, who made the quilt with me, wanted a 1960s' beach-inspired design that incorporated one of their favourite vintage images printed onto a piece of fabric placed in the centre. (Look online to find a list of local companies who will do something similar for you.) Around this they used fabric patterned with crabs and starfish, and made bird appliqués. The end result was a vivid and wonderful personal heirloom.

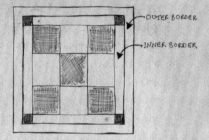

Follow the steps below to make your own unique design based on our simplified grid. The finished quilt measures 150 x 150 cm.

Fabric requirements

9 squares, each 42 x 42cm, for the central patchwork

4 strips, each 12 x 122 cm, for the inner border

4 squares, each 12 x 12 cm, for the corners of the inner border

2 strips, each 12 x 152cm, for the top and bottom of the outer border

2 strips, each 12 x 142cm, for the sides of the outer border

Wadding, 142 x 142 cm (we used organic wadding called 'warm and natural')

Backing fabric (quilting weight cotton), 142 x 142 cm

All measurements include a 1 cm seam allowance on each side.

DESIGNING YOUR QUILT

Start by laying out all the fabrics you want to incorporate into your design, and decide which work best together and how you might group them. Now make a sketch of your design (ideally drawn to scale on graph paper so that you get the proportions right). If, like Amber and Colin, you have a specific fabric that you'd like to use for the central patch but you don't have enough to make a 42 x 42 cm square, simply sew some coordinating strips to the sides of it.

MEASURING AND CUTTING OUT

Measure out each piece of fabric, marking the cutting lines with an air-soluble pen. Cut out all the pieces using either scissors or a rotary cutter with a quilter's ruler and a cutting mat (photo A).

SEWING THE PATCHWORK

Lay out the central patchwork squares in the formation you want them. Starting with the top row, place the first two pieces of fabric right sides together. Pin along the seam, about 1 cm from the edge, then machine-stitch. Remember to reverse at the start and end of the seam to prevent the stitching from unravelling. Now stitch the third square to them in the same way. Using a hot iron, press the seams open.

Repeat this process for the next two rows. You will end up with three rows of three squares stitched together.

Place the rows on a table in the formation you want. Place the top two rows right sides together, matching edges and lining up the seams. Pin together about 1 cm from the raw edges, then machine-stitch as described in step 3. Press the seams open. Repeat this step to attach the third row.

CREATING APPLIQUÉS

If you want to add any appliqué, draw your design onto a piece of paper and cut it out. Place this template on another piece of paper and draw around it, adding a margin of 1 cm all the way around. Cut out this second template.

Using the larger template, trace the design onto the back of your chosen fabric with an air-soluble pen, then cut it out (photo B). Take your smaller template and place it centrally on the back of the fabric appliqué cut-out, making sure the difference in size is the same the whole way round. Insert a few pins to hold the paper and fabric together (photo C).

HEMMING AND ATTACHING THE APPLIQUÉS

Now take a needle and thread, fold a little of the excess fabric over the edge of the paper template and sew running stitches to hold it in place (photo D). Continue around the edge, folding and stitching bit by bit, until the appliqué cut-out is completely hemmed. Iron with the paper side facing you, concentrating on the folded edges.

Carefully unpick the running stitch and peel off the paper. The fabric edges should stay folded over. Repeat this step to make as many appliqués as you want.

E

F

G

H

Pin the appliqué motif onto your chosen piece of patchwork. Using a needle and matching thread, sew around it using slipstitch (photo E).

SEWING THE INNER BORDER

Pin a corner square to one end of an inner border strip, right sides together and edges matching. Machine-stitch 1 cm from the edge. Repeat this process with each of the other inner border strips. Press the seams open.

Place one of these inner border strips on the patchwork block, right sides together, edges matching, but the corner square extending beyond the patchwork at one end. Pin in place, then machine-stitch 1 cm from the edge. Press the seam open.

Pin another prepared strip to the patchwork, placing the corner square at the short end of the strip you've just attached. Stitch and press as before. Repeat this step with the remaining strips, and finally stitch the border closed.

ATTACHING THE BACKING FABRIC

Cut the wadding and the backing fabric to size. Lay the backing, wrong side up, on a flat surface. Place the wadding on top, then cover with the patchwork, right side up (photo F). Pin this fabric sandwich together along all the seamlines, starting from the centre of the quilt and moving outwards.

SEWING THE OUTER BORDER

Take each strip of outer border fabric, fold in half along the length and press flat. Open it out and fold in 1 cm around all the raw edges. Press flat.

Pin the left-hand border and the quilt right sides together and raw edges matching. Machine-stitch 1 cm from the edge along the pressed line. Wrap the border fabric around the edge of the quilt, folding along the pressed line you made in the centre. Pin the unstitched edge to the underside of the quilt and slipstitch in place. Repeat this process for the right-hand border, then for the top and bottom borders, making sure the strips align at the corners and slipstitching the open ends closed (photo G).

QUILTING YOUR DESIGN

The quilt can be used as it stands, or you can quilt other parts of the design, either by hand or with a machine quilting attachment. Amber and Colin chose to machine-quilt between the borders, and to hand-quilt around the appliqué birds (photo H).

Reupholstered
DROP-IN SEAT PAD

Chairs are among the most versatile pieces of furniture you can have in your home. They function in practically every room in the house and are an essential addition to the vintage home. You'll find all sorts of chairs at auctions, second-hand markets and in shops. Just make sure you sit before you buy and never go on looks alone.

Simon Bell showed me how to completely overhaul a chair seat and give it a new lease of life with some basic and very beginner-friendly upholstery. It's a technique that hasn't changed much since Victorian times, and doesn't require any specialist equipment. Choose a vintage fabric that complements both your chair and your colour scheme – great fun, especially if you've already used the painting and distressing technique on it (see page 66).

Janine and Shaun, whose house we helped to transform, were going for a 1950s' look, so they chose a vintage-style floral fabric to complement the bright colours of that decade, which they had already used to paint their chairs to wonderful effect.

You will need

Chair with a 'drop-in' seat

Screwdriver (optional)

Upholstery tack lifter or pliers

Scissors

Webbing (see box overleaf)

Staple gun or upholstery tacks and hammer

Piece of 2.5 cm foam padding, to cover surface of seat frame

Spray adhesive

Interfacing, a type of wadding (see box overleaf)

Fabric (see box overleaf)

Hessian (optional)

CALCULATING YOUR MATERIALS

Webbing: *Measure the length and width of your seat frame. Let's say it's 40 cm long and 50 cm wide. Now choose a webbing width – say, 10 cm. Divide your chair measurements by the width of your webbing and this will give you the number of strips you will need to cover the seat frame: 40 ÷ 10 = 4, and 50 ÷ 10 = 5. An extra 10 cm (that's 5 cm at either end) must be added to each strip for turning under. Now do this sum:*

40 x 4 = 160 cm (width)
10 x 4 = 40 cm (extra)

Add these figures together, and you will need 200 cm (or 2 metres) of webbing to cover the chair lengthways. Repeat this sum with the width measurement to get the total amount of webbing required.

Wadding and fabric: *If you have the original seat cover, simply measure it to get the dimensions, adding an extra 5 cm all round. If you don't have the original cover, measure the width, length and height of the seat frame. Now add three times the height to the width and the length. For example, if the height is 3 cm, multiply that by 3 and you get 9 cm. Add 9 cm to the length and width measurements suggested opposite and you discover that the fabric and wadding should both be 49 x 59 cm.*

1. Turn the chair on its side and remove the seat by pushing it upwards from underneath. If it has been screwed into place, use a screwdriver to remove it, and keep the screws in a safe place for reattachment later.

2. Using an upholstery tack lifter or pair of pliers, remove the old covering from the seat. Put the fabric aside to use later as a template.

3. If the seat pad and webbing are in good condition and don't need to be replaced, go to step 7. If they do need replacing, remove the old padding and webbing plus any remaining tacks or staples in the frame.

4. Cut strips of webbing to cover the length and width of the chair, remembering to add the extra 10 cm to each strip (photo 4a). Starting at the middle on one side of the seat frame, drape the first strip of webbing across it. (It's not vital to start in the middle, but doing so makes it easier to place all your strips evenly across the frame.) Fold back 5 cm at one end of the webbing,

2

3

4a

4b

then staple or tack it in place. Do the same with the other end of the webbing, pulling it taut as you do so. Place the next length beside the first one and repeat the process until the chair is covered. Now attach the widthways strips in a similar way, but feeding them in and out of the webbing already in place to make a strong woven base for the seat pad (photo 4b).

5. Cut a piece of foam padding so that it covers the area of the seat frame. Spray the webbing with adhesive and place the foam on top. Trim off any excess.

6. Cut a piece of interfacing large enough to cover the foam and extend down to the base of the seat frame. Staple or tack to the vertical side of the frame and trim off any excess.

7. Cut your fabric to size, taking care to centre any area of pattern you'd particularly like to feature.

8. Place the fabric over the seat, then turn it over. Holding the fabric taut, start stapling or tacking it on the underside at the front and back, working outwards from the middle. Next do the sides, leaving the corners until last. At the corners, you will have to fold and possibly pleat the fabric, depending on its thickness. The most important thing all the way around the seat is to pull the fabric as tightly as possible. You might need help with this – another person keeping the fabric taut while you do the stapling or tacking.

9. For a neat finish and to hide the staples or tacks holding the fabric, cut a piece of hessian about 5 cm bigger all round than the size of your seat frame. Place it over the underside of the chair, then turn under the raw edges and staple or tack close to the folded edge.

10. Pop the covered seat pad back into the chair and screw into place again if necessary.

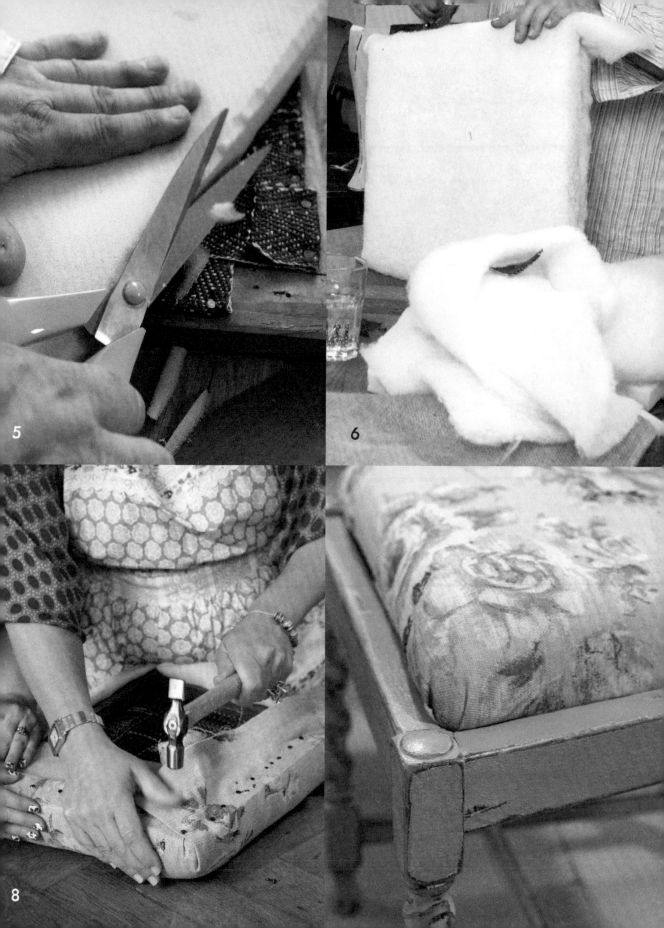

5

6

8

Baby CHANGING MAT

Working with vintage fabric is a joy, and using it to create something for a new arrival makes it extra special because you have a brand new item with a history behind it. Sewing expert Lisa Comfort helped me to make this practical and pretty changing mat, proving that bespoke beats buying any day. The finished mat measures 75 x 50 cm and has a 1 cm seam allowance all round.

You will need

77 x 52 cm piece of oil cloth

Bowl or saucer, for tracing curve

Tailor's chalk or air-soluble pen

Scissors

Pins

77 x 52 cm piece of vintage fabric

77 x 52 cm piece of wadding (preferably organic 'warm and natural' wadding, but any type can be used)

Needle and thread

½ metre of gingham, for bias binding and handle

Sewing machine

1. Place your piece of oil cloth on a table. Using an upside-down bowl or saucer as a template, draw a curve in tailor's chalk or air-soluble pen at each corner. Cut around the curves with scissors.

2. Using the oilcloth as a template, pin it to the vintage fabric and cut around the curved corners. Repeat this process with the wadding.

3. Place the oilcloth right side down, lay the wadding on it, then place the vintage fabric on top, right side facing you, to make a fabric sandwich. Securely pin all three layers together, then tack around the edges. Don't be too fussy about the stitching as it will eventually be covered by binding.

4. Now you have to make the bias binding. (Bias-cut fabric is more flexible and will bend around corners more easily.) Take the gingham and find its true bias by folding one cut edge up to the selvedge. Lightly press the fold with an iron, and that fold is the bias line of the fabric.

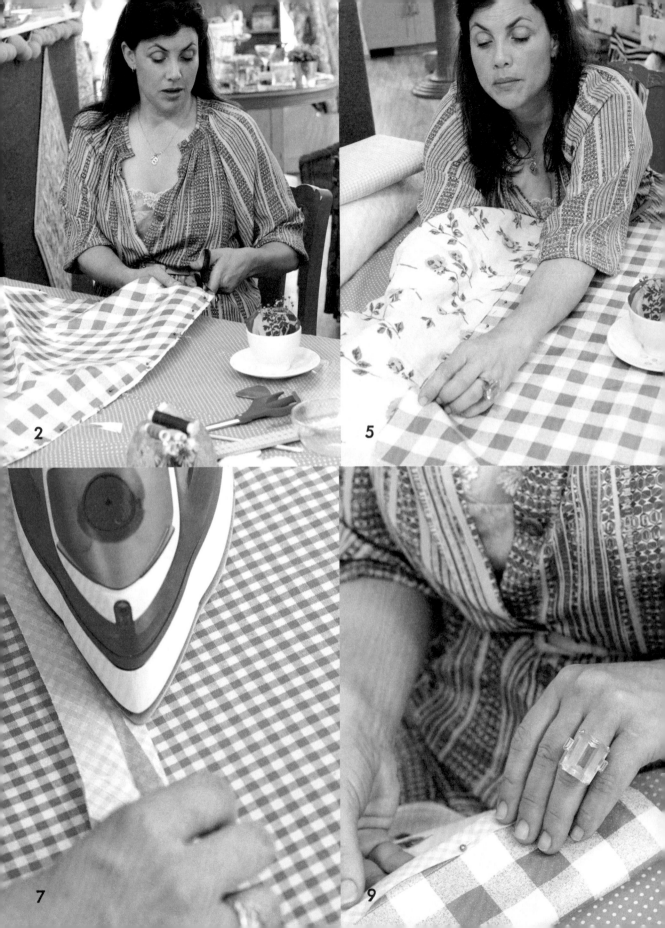

2

5

7

9

5. Using tailor's chalk or an air-soluble pen, draw diagonal lines at 5 cm intervals across the bias line you have just created. Cut along these marks so that you end up with bias strips 5 cm wide.

6. Now you need to join these strips to make one long piece of bias binding. To do this, put two strips right sides together with short edges matching. Pin, then sew across the join in running stitch. Press the seam open, taking care not to stretch the fabric. Repeat this process until you have a 2.5 metre strip.

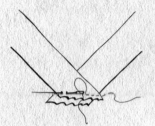

7. Take the whole strip of bias binding, fold it in half lengthways, wrong sides together, and iron flat. Turn under a 1 cm hem along one raw edge and iron flat. Leave the other edge raw for now.

8. With the vintage fabric facing you, pin the unfolded raw edge of the bias binding all around the fabric sandwich, right sides together and raw edges matching. Machine together 1 cm from the edge.

9. Fold the binding over to the underside of the sandwich so that it encases the raw edges. (Do this with the oil cloth facing you.) Pin together, making sure the line of tacking is hidden by the binding.

10. Machine stitch close to the pinned edge of the binding, sewing along your previous line of machine stitching.

11. To make a handle to tie around the changing mat when you roll it up, cut out three strips of gingham fabric 50 cm long and 6 cm wide (these do not need to be cut on the bias). Stitch the strips together to form a strip 1.5 metres long. Press the seams open, then fold the strip lengthways, wrong sides together, and iron flat. Open it up and fold the raw edges towards the crease so that they meet in the middle. Iron again.

12. Fold the strip in half lengthways again and tuck in the raw edges at top and bottom. Sew all around the strip, about 3 mm from the edge. At the beginning and end, sew a few stitches backwards and forwards to make it secure. Fold the finished mat in half, then roll up and tie with the handle.

Lino-cut BLIND

Window treatments can be a fantastic way of bringing the vintage look to your home. Sometimes, though, it's difficult to find enough vintage fabric to cover a whole window, so what do you do then? Textile designer Zeena Shah specialises in home accessories and has a fabulous solution – printing an authentic-looking period design onto plain fabric using a simple lino-cut stamp.

Lino-cut printing was pioneered by British artist Claude Flight in the years between the two world wars, so it seemed fitting to use this technique for Ellie and Nick's 1930s-inspired kitchen/diner. Ellie loves ducks and uses them in her work creating vintage-inspired homewares and fabrics, so they were a natural choice for printing onto the kitchen blind. Instructions for making your own stamp are given below, but you could buy a ready-made one if you prefer.

You will need

Pencil and paper

Scissors

Linoleum (Zeena used speed carve lino, which is easier to cut than real lino)

Lino cutter

Cutting board

Ink pad

Fabric (Zeena used 100% cotton calico, but linen also works well)

Fabric paint

Small paint tray

1. To make your lino-cut stamp, you need to make a template, so draw a design onto paper. It's best to start with something simple and large that won't be too complex to cut out. Remember, it will appear as a mirror image on the fabric, so draw your design in reverse, especially if working with letters. Ellie wanted a duck facing left, so we drew it facing right.

2. Cut out the template, place it on the lino and draw around it. Using a lino cutter, gouge away the surface surrounding the outline. The idea is to leave the duck shape standing proud so only that part will print. A top tip is to warm the lino on a radiator to make it easier to cut out.

3. When you have finished carving, test the stamp by pressing it on an ink pad and then onto paper. If the stamp picks up any ink where you don't want it, just keep carving until you are happy with the test print. Clean the ink off the lino.

4. Spread out your fabric in readiness for the printing process, then pour your fabric paint into the tray. Roll a roller in it, then run the roller over the stamp, making sure the paint is evenly distributed.

5. Gently press the stamp onto the fabric, then roll over it with a dry roller to thoroughly press in the paint. Carefully lift off the stamp, then repeat the paint and rolling process until your fabric is covered with the design. Leave to dry according to the paint manufacturer's instructions, ideally overnight.

6. To seal the design onto the fabric, iron it with a dry iron. Fabric paints are water-based, so if you go over it with a steam iron, all your hard work will be ruined. Once ironed, the fabric can be used to make your chosen window dressing.

1

2

4

5

Novelty CUSHION

Reusing vintage material from a long-forgotten garment is a wonderful way to reinvent old fabric and enjoy it once again. So don't banish old clothes to the back of the wardrobe any longer – delve in there and see what you can find. Also start looking in junk shops, charity shops and vintage shops for fabrics that could be reused to complement the look of your vintage home.

Textile designer Zeena Shah came up with a really fun way to use old fabrics by creating a novelty cushion for Iman and Heather, who wanted a vintage-style nursery for the impending arrival of their baby. Simple and easy to make from Zeena's template, the cushion can also be made to your own freestyle design. All it requires is two sides of fabric, plus any embellishments that you want to add for detail and interest. I personalised mine by adding curtains, a flower on the front door, and a chimney pot on the roof. Let your imagination run free.

You will need

Scissors

Vintage fabric assortment

Pins

Ballpoint pen

Embellishments made from felt and/or fabric scraps (optional)

Bondaweb, for stiffening fabric

Pencil

Thread, to match your fabrics

Sewing machine (optional)

Toy stuffing

Needle

1. Photocopy the template overleaf to the size you want (our house was roughly 25 x 20 cm), then cut around it and and cut out the embellishments (windows and doors).

2. Select the fabric you want for both the front and back of your cushion (the two sides don't have to be the same – in fact, it looks good if they are different). Place them right sides together, matching the straight grain, then pin together. Pin your large template to the fabric, then draw around it using a ballpoint pen. Now draw around it again, this time drawing 2 cm outside the

first line all the way around. Remove the template, then cut around the outer line on the fabric.

3. To make the embellishments, place the Bondaweb, paper side up, on the wrong side of your chosen fabric. Press with a hot iron to seal the two together and prevent fraying. Note that Bondaweb does not work well with felt, so any felt embellishments will have to be stitched in place.

4. Trace around your embellishments on the paper side of the Bondawebbed fabric, then cut them out.

5. Peel the paper backing off the fabric embellishments and position where you want them on the right side of the cushion fabric. Press with a hot iron. If you have any felt embellishments, simply pin these in place for now.

6. Thread up your sewing machine and sew around the embellishments, using any stitch you like – running stitch, zigzag, whatever your sewing machine has to offer. Note that stitching is essential for felt, but optional for other fabrics. You might like to experiment on some spare scraps before you do it for real.

7. Now pin the front and back panels of the cushion right sides together, leaving a 10 cm opening so that stuffing can be added later. Machine-stitch around the inner line that you drew on the fabric in step 2, stopping either side of the opening. Trim the fabric edges, cutting diagonally across any corners a few millimetres from the stitching line.

8. Turn the cushion right side out, using your fingers to push it into the correct shape.

9. Stuff the cushion, making it as firm or soft as you like, then close the opening by hand-stitching.

WEDDING VEIL *Canopy*

Reusing an old item in a new way gives it another lease of life and allows you to incorporate a very personal item into your room design. Like many former brides up and down the country, Janine had used her wedding veil on her big day and then kept it hidden away for the next ten years. This was a pity, because her grandmother had handstitched it when she was 90, so the piece held special significance. Happily, when Janine and Shaun decided on a *fin de siècle* look for their bedroom, it provided a great opportunity to reuse the veil in a new and romantic way. Legendary textile and interior designer Sue Timney took the veil out of the cupboard and incorporated it into a beautiful canopy to hang above the couple's bed. The best bit is that she didn't damage the veil in any way, so should Janine ever wish to pass it on to future generations for its original purpose, she still could.

The main part of the canopy consists of three layers of silk, which were dyed in toning shades of grey and silver to complement the room's colour scheme. The edges of these under-layers are bound with undyed silk ribbon to hold them together, and that ribbon provides a visual link to the bound edges of the veil, which was simply draped over the post supporting the canopy. The result was a beautiful and romantic addition to the bedroom.

Have you or another family member got a wedding veil tucked away that might be ripe for reinvention? If not, you can buy vintage wedding veils from specialist shops, and occasionally they pop up in charity shops and markets.

DYEING NOTES

• Sue used inexpensive Dylon fabric dye, which is widely available in high street shops, supermarkets and online. The water for the dye was heated to 40°C.
• Always follow the packet instructions because the type of container used (plastic or metal), or even a slight difference in water temperature, can affect the outcome. • Adding salt to the mixture helps the fabric to become more porous and take the dye better. • Dyeing fabric is a real art, and with practice you can create unique colours and finishes. Sue mixed two colours to get the colour Janine wanted for her canopy. • Always do a test on a small amount of fabric first to check that you are happy with the colour, and make adjustments as necessary.

CALCULATING YOUR MATERIALS

The veil used can be any size because it is simply draped over the post supporting the finished canopy.

For underneath the veil, you need both gauzy silk tulle and slightly heavier habotai silk (often used for lining men's jackets), plus silk ribbon for binding the visible edge of the canopy. If your budget doesn't extend to these materials, you can use cheaper tulle, netting or other synthetics for this project, but they tend to be stiffer and therefore will not hang in the same way as natural silks.

To work out how much fabric you need, start by finding the central point on the headboard, then mark how high above that point you want the canopy to hang. Measure from the high point down to the corner of the headboard, where the canopy will be tied back, then measure from there down to the floor. Add the figures together, multiply by two, and that gives the total length needed for each under-layer and the ribbon (you can add extra if you want your canopy to drape on the floor as Janine's does). Janine's bed was king-sized, so Sue used 12 metres of silk tulle (6 metres for each layer), 6 metres of habotai silk, and 6 metres of ribbon.

REPAIRING AND WASHING THE VEIL

If your veil is an antique or made from an unusual material, consult an expert for advice before you attempt to repair or wash it. A local dressmaker, alterations shop or bridal shop will be able advise you.

If you don't require expert advice, use a fine needle and silk thread to repair any holes in the veil, making your stitches as small and discreet as possible.

Once the repairs have been made, gently wash the veil in lukewarm water with mild soap; never use harsh detergents. Rinse thoroughly, gently squeeze out the excess water by hand (do not spin), then hang up to dry.

DYEING THE UNDER-LAYERS

Thoroughly soak each length of tulle and habotai silk in cool water. Meanwhile, wearing rubber gloves and an apron, prepare your chosen dye according to the manufacturer's instructions (photo A). When it's ready, test-dye a scrap of each fabric to check that it is the colour you want. When you're happy that the colour is correct, gently squeeze the excess water out of your soaked fabrics and place them in the dye. Stir continuously with a large metal spoon for about 15 minutes, or according to the packet instructions. After that, leave for 30 minutes, stirring occasionally.

Remove the dyed fabric with tongs and rinse in cold water until the water runs clear. Finally, wash in warm water and hang up to dry away from direct heat and sunlight.

Once the fabric is dry, it can be steam-ironed, but the iron itself must not directly touch the fabric. Always press through a damp cloth (photo B). Take your time over this as it's all too easy to burn the delicate fabric.

STITCHING THE RIBBON TO THE TULLE

Fold the ribbon in half along its length and iron flat. Place the silk fabrics on top of each in any combination you want and align the edges. Tuck the front edge of the three fabrics inside the folded ribbon and pin together along the whole length. This bound edge of the canopy will be visible, so take your time to do it accurately and neatly. Tack together, then machine-stitch with matching thread (photo C).

HANGING THE CANOPY

Steam-iron the joined fabrics before you start the hanging process, pressing them through a damp cloth to avoid any risk of burning.

Sue used a large vintage yarn spool to hang the canopy from. You can source something similar from second-hand shops or online. Attach the spool to the wall at your chosen centre point above the bed. Hang the silk layers over the spool, with the ribbon edge facing outwards. Drape the fabrics gracefully, then use ribbon to fasten them to either side of the headboard. Finally, place the veil over the spool, ruffling it to make it look beautiful (photo D).

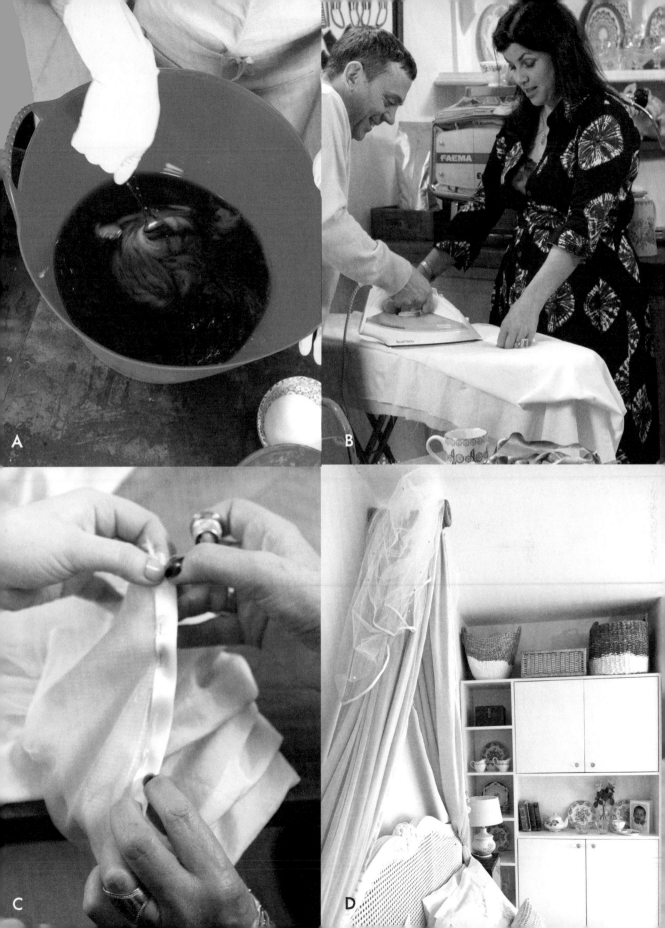

A

B

C

D

FINISHING
TOUCHES

Your almost completed room may look lovely, but it is the final flourishes – the finishing touches – that will give it the wow factor. They are essential to achieving the look you want, and I believe that the process of adding them is the most enjoyable part of decorating – the part where you can really show off your flair.

Finishing touches must be your own, reflecting your personality and taste, so I can't possibly tell you what to buy. All I can say is that the best and only good reason to display something in your home is that you have fallen in love with it, looking at it makes you happy and, despite any imperfections it may have, you still want it.

Be true to your instincts and you will notice themes starting to develop, such as colours you always go for and patterns you are drawn to. If you want a particular period look, that can also influence your choices, but always remember to trust your own sense of style and don't let anyone else put you off.

Your own hand-crafted pieces will be the finishing touches that lift your decor beyond the ordinary and make it 'sing'. It is enormously satisfying to see charming objects you have made with your own hands decorating your house. Using vintage materials or traditional crafting techniques from your chosen period are a great way to pull off a fabulous vintage style. The projects in this chapter will help you to do this and will, I hope, encourage you to try out new crafts or revisit old ones. See how we found unexpected beauty in weaving natural willow placemats on page 170, or learn how to complete your art deco look with gilding on page 177. The possibilities are huge and the challenge thrilling, so come with me and I'll show you the way.

HOW TO PUT IT ALL TOGETHER

By this point I hope you've got a good idea of how to find, buy and do up vintage furniture successfully, and how to use soft furnishings to great effect. As far as your other buys are concerned – those lovely bits and pieces you've been gradually accumulating as you trawl charity shops, markets and auction houses – the task now is to work them into your scheme imaginatively and get them to look good. My aim here is to show you the basics, which you can then use as inspiration to create your own very personal vintage look.

Before we get started, a word of advice: don't be precious about your finishing touches. The rough and tumble of daily life means that things you've carefully arranged will get moved and wrinkled, maybe even hidden or broken. I like things to be neat and tidy in my home, but I'm aware that it's a place for living in too. With a houseful of boys, big and little, I would drive myself absolutely mad if I constantly stressed about things being in their place. Don't get obsessed with the details being in perfect order. You can spend hours plumping cushions to perfection, but there will always be someone who sits down and squashes them. It's better to have a lived-in home than an untouched work of art where no one feels comfortable.

WHAT TO DISPLAY

Always use pieces that make you happy. Some things hold a sentimental value that you just can't explain. They might be ugly, odd, or completely the wrong colour for your room, but your attachment to them is unbreakable. Display every piece with pride. A crinoline lady for hiding the spare toilet roll might not be everyone's cup of tea, but if it's your special family heirloom and brings back memories of your grandmother, put it out. This also applies to the things that someone else in your house loves, although maybe you don't. Have tolerance!

Add the unexpected. I really love injecting a bit of humour or a surprise element into my rooms. Putting an unexpected item into a room lifts it out of the ordinary and creates a talking point. It could be something unusual, such as a tailor's dummy, or something out of scale with the rest of the room, such as a very large plant or a giant lamp. And things don't get much more surprising than the crochet jellyfish we made in vivid 1960s' colours (see page 154). Like a space-age chair in a medieval castle, it simply isn't what you would expect to see. Look out for talking-point pieces whenever you're second-hand shopping, but do remember that if a piece is designed to grab a lot of attention, it is doubly important for you to love it.

Create collections. Displays of vintage items are really key when you're creating a vintage look. They bring a small slice of history into your home, evoke times gone by and provide a lovely focus. They can also inject colour, texture and pattern – all essentials to creating a homely space. What I love about collections is that each one is unique. Nobody else in the world will have the same collection as you.

Collections can be made up of just about anything: vintage jelly moulds, commemorative tea towels, old telescopes, vintage keys, biscuit tins, children's toys, pincushions, retro suitcases – you name it, you can make a collection of it.

Collectables don't have to be valuable items in monetary terms; they just need to be special to you. It takes only one object that captures your interest to start the collecting bug. If you catch yourself searching for pieces similar to your first buy and secretly planning to add one or two at the next opportunity, the bug has bitten you. You will find yourself adding to your collection every time you go second-hand shopping.

Collecting involves the buzz of finding a treasure where you sometimes least expect, or experiencing the thrill of the chase. The point is that you can't rush a collection; you have to build it over time.

If you are looking for specific items for your collection, keep your ear to the ground and your eyes peeled at all times. Rope your friends and families into the search too. The Internet, of course, has transformed collecting and made it far easier to find vintage items. Whether you adore 1940s' floral table linen or your passion is for art deco clocks, regularly check the large, general auction sites online, as well as specialist sites, and you'll be sure to find what you are looking for.

HOW TO DISPLAY COLLECTIONS

Display your vintage collections and best finds with care. It is horribly easy for them to look like junk if they are scattered randomly around the house. Similarly, if you spread them thinly around a room on tables, shelves and mantelpieces, they can look unconnected from each other, especially if you have a lot of small objects. This final stage of dressing a room is when you should be aiming to bring the look together, and grouping similar objects is one of the simplest ways to do this. For example, a collection of old cameras from different eras looks great displayed on shelves in the living room; piled up packs of vintage cards make a lovely display on your hall table; and a row of retro-style jugs on a kitchen windowsill looks both pretty and practical. You get the idea – it's really simple!

When making displays, think about grouping items by shared colour or shape. You could also put similar materials or textures together. Take time to experiment with different looks and you will start to see patterns and themes emerging that you can build on. But what if you have a disparate collection of

Opposite: *Grouping similarly coloured items together creates the appearance of a collection, and gives a sense of unity to disparate objects.*

items – vases, jugs and bottles, for example – that look unrelated? A simple idea to make them look as though they belong together is to spray-paint them the same colour (see page 152 for this technique).

One word of warning: don't fill every square inch of the room with collections or it will start to look like a jumble sale. Know when to stop.

SHELF AND CABINET DISPLAYS

Simply shoving things onto shelves and into cabinets is just not good enough. Look at these display areas and ask yourself if they could be made more attractive and show off your possessions to greater advantage. They can offer the vintage enthusiast a wonderful decorating opportunity, so please make the most of them. (See the memory box display on page 78.)

I love books and, of course, these naturally belong on shelves. Whether you like them to be randomly placed, strictly alphabetical, arranged by subject, or by the colour of the spines (this can look really effective if you've got the time to do it), the choice is yours. It looks great to arrange books both vertically and in horizontal piles on the shelves, perhaps in blocks of colour. It may be necessary to remove the dust covers to get the best effect, but please keep them somewhere safe, even if they are old and quite tatty. Dust jackets can add enormously to the value of vintage books.

Don't limit your shelves just to books. Mix other bits and bobs in with them too. Use the horizontal piles of books as platforms for knick-knacks, grouping small things together for greater impact, and leaving space for larger items alongside. This process takes time and thought, but ultimately the effort is worth it because the results can really set the room alight.

TABLE DISPLAYS

Coffee tables are feature of many living rooms, so I think they deserve a special mention. Of course they are functional, so don't get rid of the coasters or anything else used on a regular basis, but use a bit of the surface to enjoy some of the wonderful pieces you have collected and let them help to set the tone of your chosen vintage era. Start your arrangement with four simple things:

1. Something tall, such as a vase or candlesticks
2. Something quirky that expresses your personality (perhaps a novelty paperweight)
3. Flowers or a houseplant
4. Books or magazines

Opposite: *Here's a lovely arrangement of colourful plates and mugs. The blue and white theme works really well.*

Once you have gathered these items, let your imagination do the rest. These rules can also be applied to other tables and surfaces, including chests of drawers and radiator covers.

WALL DISPLAYS

If you take only one thing away from this guide, please let it be the importance of decorating your walls. I often find that people spend hours and hours planning their rooms, but forget about the walls and leave them bare. Please don't do that.

Many things can be hung on the walls to brilliant effect, so don't think I am suggesting you start an expensive art collection. Far from it. You can frame and display old certificates, family photographs, postcards and even letters. Vintage maps of your area (start collecting now!) would also make a lovely display, as would an arrangement of decorative plates. Just about anything can decorate your walls. Page 182 shows a simple way of displaying children's artwork and vintage finds by pegging them to a length of wire. And don't forget the trusty pinboard. Give it a vintage make-over (see page 180), then use it for an ever-changing display of interesting items.

HOW TO HANG PICTURES

The one thing I hate more than blank walls is seeing a single lonely picture in acres of space, often hanging so high up that nobody can see it. Really, it doesn't have to be like that. There are loads of different ways that you can hang pictures. Here are some ideas and methods to inspire you.

Clear your floor and lay out everything you have to put up on the walls. Now try out various arrangements of your items before you start banging nails and screws into the wall. Bear in mind that small pieces work well when grouped together, whereas larger items might need to stand alone to look their best. Experimenting will point you in the right direction.

Pictures, plates and mirrors look great all mixed up together, but you could also hang them in separate groups. For example, putting lots of vintage mirrors together on one wall can be really effective. I helped our contributors Amber and Colin hang two vintage mirrors above a dresser, and the impact was so much greater than we could have achieved with just one.

The same applies to hanging pictures as it does to displaying collections – look for colours, patterns and textures that complement each other and work

Opposite: *Alignment is very important when hanging pictures, particularly when they are different sizes.*

well together. If you can't make this work to your satisfaction, remember that similar-coloured frames will unite disparate pieces.

Once you are feeling pretty confident that you have arrived at the best layout and grouping for your pictures, I strongly recommend the following step before you make a single hole in the wall. Take a large piece of paper and draw around the outline of each picture. Cut out the shapes and you have templates of everything that might go on the wall. Using non-marking Blu-Tack, hang your templates on the wall where you think they should go. This gives you the freedom to move them around until you have the right grouping and spacing. It sounds like a lot of effort, but it is worth putting in the groundwork before you start hammering holes into your walls. Note that this is really a two-person job, so rope someone in to help.

TIPS FOR DISPLAYING PICTURES

• Hang them at eye level so they can be seen – that's the whole point!

• Pictures also look good if they are close to a piece of furniture. Arranging a group of them just above a sofa or side table, for example, avoids that disembodied, floating-high-up-the-wall look.

• If hanging a large picture or mirror above a mantelpiece, keep the bottom edge of it close to the mantel.

• Imagine a line down the middle of your wall, splitting it in half. Hang your pictures on either side of that line, balancing each side up symmetrically. Make sure you use a tape measure and spirit level to give this look the precision it needs.

• If you prefer a more central arrangement, try putting the largest picture in the middle of the wall and placing smaller pictures around it, going outwards and upwards. This type of arrangement looks good over a sofa, sideboard or any large focal point in your room, and works well when your picture frames are a variety of shapes and sizes.

HOW TO DISPLAY EVERYDAY ITEMS

Now you've got your vintage items sorted, the question of what to do with your everyday things is bound to be asked. There are certain items in the home — remote controls, boxes of tissues and keys, to mention but a few — that can't just be kept in drawers all the time. You have to live! Try out some of the following tips to turn them into vintage styling opportunities.

Let's consider the bedside table. On mine I always have hand cream, an alarm clock, my mobile phone and current book. Often there's a glass of water or cup of tea hanging around too. Then there are the photo frames, trinket boxes and other knick-knacks I like to keep nearby. It all adds up to an awful lot of stuff, but if these items are placed on a tray, they become a display rather than a random assortment of things that have been left lying around. (Try découpaging the tray with vintage paper or old photographs for a lovely vintage twist — see page 63.)

Another idea for decluttering your bedside table or dresser is to create a beautiful stand for your jewellery. Just get some vintage plates of different sizes and glue eggcups or teacups between them (like the pedestals on a cake stand). Or make your very own trinket box (see page 151).

Side tables in the living room can be treated in a similar way to bedside tables. Keep your essential everyday stuff neatly contained on a pretty tray, and arrange a collection of, say, pillboxes or powder compacts alongside it.

Vintage bowls can bring wonderful order to the disparate stuff that always seems to gather in the bathroom. Use them for holding toothbrushes, soap, jewellery or cotton wool. In the living room a small wicker basket will keep your remote controls tidy, and you won't have to spend hours looking for them down the side of the sofa. (See page 178 for how to dip-dye baskets.)

Even the most mundane items can be turned into an opportunity for a finishing touch, and tissue boxes certainly fall into this category. I know some people think the idea of covering them is twee and outdated, but I don't. If this book has taught you anything, it's to bring into your home what you love, so if you like them too, go for it. The covers can easily be made from vintage lace or fabric. Just cut and sew four side pieces to a top piece in which you have created a slit and there you have it — a fantastically easy way to turn a mundane item into a crafter's dream. That's what finishing touches are all about.

2

4

Trinket BOXES

Every girl's bedroom tends to be filled with lots of trinkets and pretty things, no matter what age we are. And of course we all need something to keep these little treasures in. I spent a girlie afternoon with Richard's daughters, Daisy and Amy, plus their schoolfriends, showing them this trinket box craft. It's perfect for whiling away a rainy afternoon, and a super way to get the kids (well, the girls anyway) involved in the decoration of their vintage room.

Buy cheap wooden boxes from craft shops or, even better, pick them up at car boot sales or in second-hand shops and markets. Their appearance doesn't matter, as long as you like their shape and size, because you can totally transform them with beads and buttons (also readily available in all the usual places). This craft really is child's play – just paint, pick and stick!

You will need

Cloth or plastic sheet

Wooden box

Coloured paint

2 paintbrushes, 1 for paint
and 1 for glue

PVA glue

Selection of embellishments – beads,
buttons, glitter, shells, feathers, etc.

1. Prepare the area you are going to work in by covering it with a cloth or plastic sheet.

2. Paint the outside of your box in any colour or finish you like, then set aside until completely dry.

3. Once the paint is dry, apply some PVA glue to the box, a smallish area at a time, and stick down some of your chosen embellishments. You can make the arrangement as complex or as simple as you like.

4. Allow the glued embellishments to dry, then paint a layer of PVA glue all over them to give a protective seal. This also stops them falling off and gives a nice shiny finish. Leave to dry, then use and display.

Spray-painting OBJECTS

Here's a crafty way to transform those objects you buy at car boot sales and the like but can't always fit into your vintage scheme when you get them home: spray-painting. It can bring dowdy and old-fashioned items bang up to date, and give everyday objects a new lease of life. Amber and Colin, for example, sprayed an old brown bottle and transformed it into a quirky vase. Just remember that items with a hard surface, especially non-glazed ceramics, respond best to spraying. Slick or glazed surfaces should be sanded lightly before spraying to help the paint stick, otherwise it will simply run off.

You will need

Plastic sheet or old newspapers, to protect your spraying area

Protective clothing

Rubber gloves

Face mask (optional)

Your chosen object to spray

Fine sandpaper (optional)

Stick, for holding objects while spraying (optional)

Spray paint: 1 can in matt white (optional) and 1 can in your chosen top colour, whatever finish you like (just make sure it's suitable for the surface of your object, as explained above)

1. Cover the spraying area with a plastic sheet or old newspapers. Don your protective clothing, gloves and face mask.

2. Make sure your object is clean and free of dust, especially if you have sanded it as described above to give the paint a better surface to stick to. It's a good idea to start by applying a coat of white paint because it provides a good base for the top coat, but it's not essential. Hold up your object, either in your hand or on the end of a stick, and spray the white paint over it, going from left to right in short strokes about 15 cm from the object. This stops the paint from gathering and dripping. Leave to dry (this will take at least 20 minutes).

3. Once the object is completely dry, apply your chosen colour over the white, using the same technique as in step 2, and leave to dry. If you would like to create a deliberate drip effect (as we did with the brown bottle), don't apply the first layer of white paint. Simply spray with your chosen colour at a distance closer than 15 cm: this means that the paint will gather and drip.

Crocheted JELLYFISH

Quirky and fun, this project was designed by Sue Timney, and it's a simple introduction for anyone new to crochet. Make it in bright colours to reflect the Swinging Sixties, as we have here, or in shades that reflect the vintage period you love.

Two simple stitches are used in this project – chain or slipstitch for the tentacles, and double crochet stitch for the body, which looks like a domed head. If you're new to crochet, start with the tentacles, and then progress to the body. Once you've got the hang of the stitches involved, you can easily go freestyle and make other projects of your own devising.

You will need

Ball of yarn (it should be slightly thicker than the bigger hook)

2 crochet hooks: 7 mm and 6 mm

Scissors

Tapestry needle, for weaving loose ends into the finished work

Nylon fishing line, for hanging up the finished jellyfish

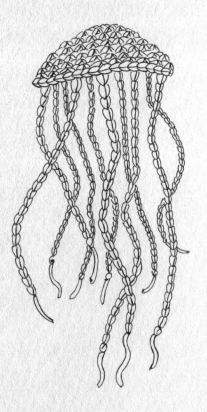

1. Start by making a slipknot. To do this, make a small loop in the yarn, leaving the loose end about 15 cm long. Insert the 7 mm hook into the loop, catch the ball end of the yarn and pull it back through the loop. Pull both ends of the yarn to tighten the knot.

2. Hold the yarn in the opposite hand to the hook. It's a good idea to wrap the yarn around your index finger and hold it between your thumb and middle finger so that it's at right angles to the hook. This way you are holding it firmly, and when you pull it through the loop, it stays in the lip of the hook. Put the hook into the loop you have just made, catch the yarn and pull it through. This is called a chain stitch. Repeat this stitch as many times as you like, depending on how long you want each tentacle to be. Mine were roughly 30 cm long, but every tentacle can be a slightly different length.

3. To fasten off, complete the final stitch, then cut the working yarn about 15 cm long and pull it through the last loop on the hook. Tighten the yarn to close the loop (the 15 cm length will later be used for attaching it to the body). Now you have a tentacle! Repeat steps 1–3 to make as many tentacles as you wish.

4. To make the body, follow steps 1 and 2 to create a foundation row or chain with 4 chain stitches.

5. Now you are going to join these together to form the middle of the jellyfish. With your fourth chain stitch still on the hook, put your hook through the first chain stitch you made (5a) and pull the yarn through. The chain should now be joined in a circle (5b).

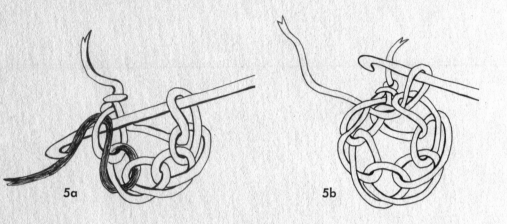

5a

5b

6. You are now going to use double crochet stitch around the chain to form the body of the jellyfish. With the last chain stitch still on your hook, take the hook through the centre of the circle you have just created and pull the yarn through. There are now two loops on the hook (6a). Wrap the yarn around the hook and pull it through both loops on the hook. This leaves one loop on the hook and completes the first double crochet stitch (6b).

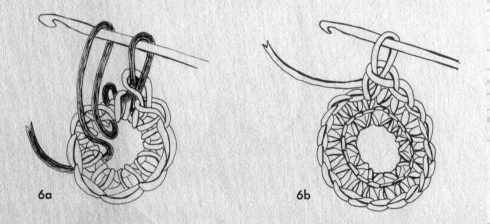

6a

6b

7. Now put the hook into the second chain stitch from the hook so you've again got two loops on the hook. Wrap the yarn around the hook and pull it through both loops. This is the second double crochet stitch. Repeat this a further eight times, making a total of ten times for the first row of the jellyfish body.

8. To make the next row, instead of putting the hook through the centre circle of the jellyfish's body as per step 6, put the hook through the first stitch of the row above and repeat the process for the double crochet stitch. To make the jellyfish body grow, you need to increase the number of stitches. To do this, every second stitch, work into the same stitch twice.

9. When you have reached the desired size for your jellyfish (mine was about 10 cm in diameter), crochet one full row of double crochet stitch with no increase. After that, to create the 'lip' around the edge of the jellyfish, you need to decrease by skipping every second stitch for three rows.

10. To fasten off, complete the final stitch, then cut the working yarn about 15 cm long and pull it through the last loop on the hook. Tighten the yarn to close the loop and weave the loose end into the inside of the jellyfish body with a tapestry needle.

11. Now it's time to attach the tentacles. Using the 6 mm hook, find a loop on the underside of the body and use the hook to pull the yarn end of a tentacle through it. Tie a knot to hold it firmly in place. Weave any loose ends into the body with a tapestry needle. Trim off any excess yarn.

12. Finally, thread a short length of nylon fishing line through the top of the domed body and tie in a loop to secure. Now hang up your jellyfish wherever you like.

Hand-moulded PLATE

The kitchen is one room in the house that really can't do without modern technology and appliances, so it's the small details you add that give it a vintage style and feel. Displaying collections and pretty things in the kitchen and dining area is a real must. If you are lucky enough to have a dresser or open shelves, make sure you fill them with all your vintage finds and vintage-inspired handmade items.

This lovely hand-moulded plate is an easy introduction to making your own pottery, and you can design your own vintage-inspired look for it. Ellie and Nick were after a 1930s-inspired kitchen and dining room, and their plates really reflect that era, when Clarice Cliff and Susie Cooper were prominent names in British pottery design.

Ceramics expert Richard Miller took Ellie, Nick and me through the process of hand-moulding plates, and then took them away to fire in his kiln. You can easily do this too: just search online for a friendly local potter and ask if they can fire your plate in their kiln.

You will need

Apron

Old sheet or cloth to cover your work surface

3 kg white stoneware clay

Sharp knife and cutting board

2 wooden battens, about 8 mm thick, placed either side of your clay when rolling out, to ensure an even thickness (optional)

Rolling pin

Plate mould (professional moulds are made of plaster, but at home you can mould your clay inside an ordinary dinner plate)

Turning or banding wheel (similar to an icing turntable, optional)

3–4 cm paintbrush (for water)

Potter's kidney (smoothing tool, optional)

Newsprint, pencil and scissors, to create your design (optional)

Sponge

Slips (liquid clays in various colours)

2–3 cm soft paintbrush (for slip)

Hairdryer (optional)

Needle (optional)

Fine artist's brush (optional)

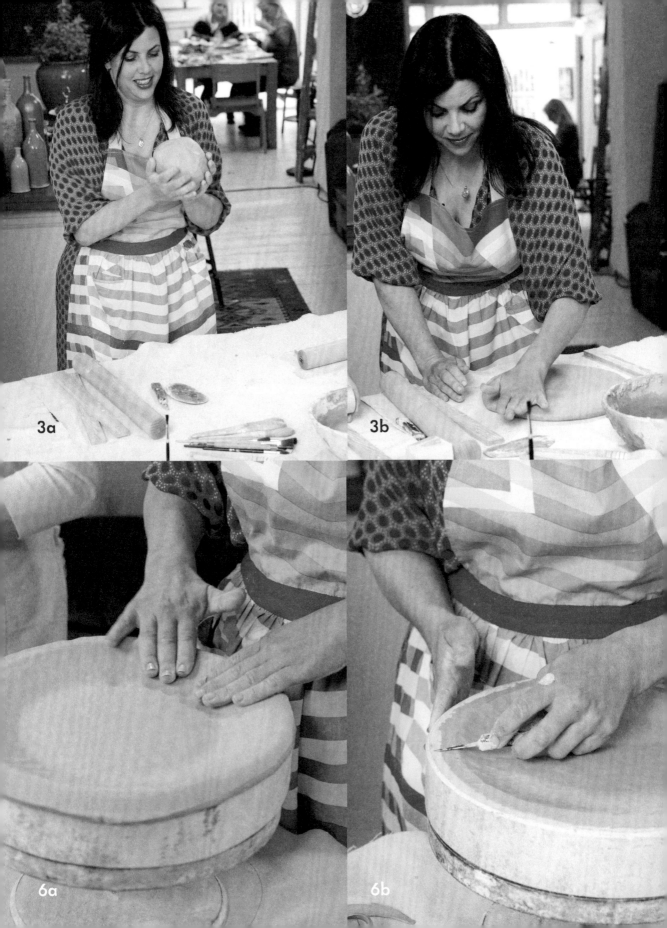

7a

7b

8

9

1. Making pottery can be messy, so do wear an apron, or old clothes that you don't mind getting dirty. Cover your work surface with an old sheet or cloth.

2. Take your clay and slam it onto your work surface, then knead and beat it to remove any air bubbles and make it smooth. This process is called 'wedging' and is done to prevent the clay from breaking in the kiln when fired. There is no set time for wedging; in fact, it varies for each piece of clay – sometimes as little as 5 minutes, and maybe as much as 15. You have to keep checking whether the air bubbles have gone, and to do this you simply cut the clay in half. Any air bubbles will appear as small holes. If you find some, keep wedging until the clay is hole-free.

3. Form the clay into a football shape, then place it on your work surface and press it firmly to flatten it a bit (photos 3a, 3b). Put a wooden batten on either side of the clay, then use a rolling pin to roll out the clay until it is slightly bigger than your plate mould and the same thickness as the battens (about 1 cm). Turn it now and again during this process, moving the battens apart as the clay stretches, until it is nice and flat on both sides.

4. Take your mould, turn it upside down and put it on top of the clay. Using a sharp knife, cut around the mould about 2–3 cm outside the edge.

5. Turn the mould the right way up and, if you have a turning wheel, put it on top, making sure it is centred. If you don't have a wheel, just stand the mould on your covered work surface (the cloth will stop it slipping around). Brush the mould with water, then press the sheet of clay into it. This is called 'slumping'.

6. Continue working the clay into the mould by pressing with your fingers and using long strokes to keep it an even thickness throughout (photo 6a). It must not be thinner at the rim. Once you are happy that your plate is correctly moulded, trim the edge with a sharp knife (photo 6b). To get rid of any unwanted marks or impressions, smooth a few drops of water over the clay using your fingers or a potter's kidney.

7. While the clay is still in the mould, it can be personalised with your own design. You can do this freehand with a knife, lightly scoring patterns, names, dates or whatever you like into the clay. Alternatively, cut out simple paper shapes, such as stripes, stars or spots, position them on the clay, then dab them with a damp sponge so that they stay in place (photos 7a, 7b).

8. Now choose one or more coloured slips to apply to your design, taking inspiration from your chosen era. You can use as many as you like, but it's probably best to keep things simple until you get more practice. Using a soft paintbrush, start applying the slip in the middle and work outwards. Don't be afraid to load up your paintbrush – the more slip you use, the more vibrant the colour will be.

9. If using a hairdryer to dry the slip, work it around the plate for 5 minutes or so to give a nice even finish, then peel off the paper shapes (if you used them) by gently lifting a corner of each one with a needle or the tip of a sharp knife, being careful not to mark the clay. Alternatively, leave to dry naturally, removing the paper strips after 10 minutes, then leaving the plate to dry further for 30–60 minutes. Once the drying is complete, you can apply different coloured slips to the revealed pattern if you want, but dry each colour before applying the next one. The extra colours are best applied with a fine artist's brush so that they don't overlap with previous ones.

10. You can now gently remove the plate from the mould: it should come away easily. Leave to dry out for three days, then place it back in the mould and take to your local pottery or ceramic shop, who will be able to add a clear glaze (matt or shiny, as you prefer) and fire it in the kiln.

Tiled SPLASHBACK

Potter Richard Miller helped Ellie and Nick make some gorgeous pottery plates to display on their dresser (see page 160), and he also made some beautiful tiles to complete their 1930s' country kitchen look. I went along to show them how to put up the tiles, and here I share my secrets with you. As they say, it's all in the planning...

You will need

Tape measure	Notched spreader
Pencil and paper	Sponge
Tiles	Spirit level
Camera (optional)	2 mm spacers
Coarse sandpaper	Grout plus float for spreading it
Trowel	Grout finisher
Tile adhesive	Soft cloth

1. Measure the space on the wall where you want to put your splashback and work out how many tiles you will have for the height and width. Ours was six tiles high and five tiles wide. Draw a rough sketch of the tile arrangement; it doesn't have to be to scale, but should be large enough to make notes on, as required in step 3.

2. Lay all your tiles out on the floor, take a good look at them, then arrange them as you'd like to see them on the wall. It's best to start from the bottom centre and work your way out and up. Play around with the arrangement until you are happy with it.

3. Starting from the bottom left-hand corner, work along the rows from left to right and pencil a number on the back of each tile. Also mark this number on the appropriate square of your sketch. (You could take a photograph of the layout if you like.)

4. Prepare the wall for the tiles by rubbing it with sandpaper. This will help the adhesive to stick. Using a trowel, spread tile adhesive onto the wall, covering an area no more than 1 metre square because you don't want the adhesive to dry before you get all the tiles up. Go over the adhesive with a notched spreader, working from left to right (photos 4a, 4b). The ridges created will help to get an equal quantity of adhesive behind each tile. Wipe off any splashes of adhesive with a damp sponge.

5. With your sketch nearby for reference, position the first tile on the wall at the bottom left-hand corner, checking it is straight with a spirit level. Place the second tile to the right of the first one, and the third tile above the first one, again checking with a spirit level that they are straight. Place spacers at the corners where tiles intersect to make sure they are equally spaced. Push the spacers well into the adhesive so that they can be grouted over. Continue adding tiles, referring to your sketch and the numbers on the back of the tiles to make sure you are placing them correctly. When you have tiled the whole area, leave the adhesive to set. This usually takes around 24 hours, but check the manufacturer's instructions as different brands vary.

6. When the adhesive is completely dry, it's time to fill in the gaps between the tiles. Using a float and working quickly, spread grout all over the tiles in long strokes (photo 6a). Once the grout has hardened slightly (and it does this pretty quickly), pull a grout finisher along it in long, smooth movements to give it a nice neat finish. Wipe any excess grout off the tiles with a damp sponge (photo 6b).

7. Leave the grout to dry according to the manufacturer's instructions, but for no less than 24 hours. Once it's dry, polish up your tiles with a soft cloth.

4a

4b

6a

6b

Willow PLACEMATS

During the 1930s, homes were being built at a rate of knots all over the UK. People were moving in droves out to suburbia and into lovely new semis and detached properties, where the kitchen, as now, was the heart of the home. Ellie and Nick wanted to create their own warm and friendly 1930s-inspired country kitchen and dining space, and part of that period look was achieved with basketry, a popular craft in their chosen decade.

It's well known that I love basketry in my home, so I enlisted the help of wonderful willow weaver Eddie Glew, who designed these fantastic willow placemats to grace Ellie and Nick's kitchen table. I really enjoyed the experience of making them and I am sure you will too.

You will need (per placemat)

About 30 willow rods, for weaving (depending on the size of your placemat), plus 6 rods for the base

Large container, for soaking the willow (this could be done in the bath)

Secateurs

Ruler

Bodkin (a pointed handtool, not the sewing variety)

Cutting mat

1. Put all the willow in a large container of water and leave to soak until supple – this usually takes about a day.

2. Using secateurs, cut six willow sticks from the butt (thick) end of the willow to make the base for your placemat. The length of the sticks will determine the size of your placemat, so cut accordingly. My sticks were around 30 cm long.

3. Using a bodkin, and leaning on a cutting mat if you wish, split a hole in the middle of three of the sticks. The hole should be just big enough to pass your other three sticks through. With the bodkin still through the three split rods, insert the three other sticks vertically through the holes to create a cross formation. You now have the base around which to weave the rods.

4. Take two rods and put the tips (the thin end) into the base sticks from the left-hand side. Push through until around 5 cm are poking through on the right. Where the sticks cross, start wrapping these two rods around the centre in a clockwise direction. This will form the centre square.

5. Continue wrapping one rod under and one rod over the first side of the cross. When the rods meet, cross the bottom rod over the top rod to hold it in place. Now the bottom rod is on top and the top rod is at the bottom. Repeat this process until you have gone right around the cross three times.

6. Now spread out the six base sticks to make 12 spokes (photo 6a) and continue weaving the rods over and under each spoke (as per step 5) until you have made a large circle for your placemat (photo 6b). Weaving the rods in pairs like this will give a strong and balanced base.

7. When you get towards the end of a rod, simply add a new one underneath the old one and continue weaving. If the rod you are using finishes on the butt end, start with the butt end of the new piece; similarly, a tip end should be continued with the tip end of a new piece. When you get within three or four rows of completing the mat, finish your weaving with the tip end of the willow and tuck it under a spoke.

8. Now you are going to make a border to finish the mat. Add in the butt end of a weaving rod at each spoke by placing it under the spoke. Now put it on top of two spokes, then under one spoke, working each rod around the circle this way in a clockwise direction. Finish each rod underneath (which will be the bottom on the placemat). Repeat this process at every spoke in the circle. Trim any excess willow underneath with secateurs, always cutting at an angle for a lovely finish.

3

4

6a

6b

FELT *Garland*

Layering textures with fabrics and materials is a must in every vintage home. This easy-to-make felt garland is a really pretty project for doing just that. In the spirit of reusing and recycling, textile designer Selina Rose donated some felt off-cuts left over from her work, but you can make your own by using paper templates and cutting out the felt yourself. Sewing the shapes together with invisible thread is a great way of creating an alternative to bunting, and looks fantastic in a kid's bedroom.

You will need

Paper and pencil

Scissors or a craft knife

Pins

Felt (Selina uses 100% wool felt 3 mm thick, but any type can be used)

Cutting mat

Sewing machine

Invisible thread

Steel hole puncher

Hammer

1. Sketch out on paper the shapes you want for the garland. Cut them out and you now have your templates. You can have as many different shapes and colours as you like in your garland, but large, simple shapes work best. Flowers, butterflies and leaves, for example, are easy to draw and cut out.

2. Pin your template(s) onto the felt and cut out as many as you like. My garland was 2.5 metres long, but you can make yours any length you wish.

3. Machine-stitch along the middle of the first shape from side to side, then feed the second shape in as close as possible to the first one (photo 3a). You don't want the pieces to overlap, but neither do you want any gaps, so take your time to get this step right. Repeat with the rest of the shapes until your garland is complete (photo 3b).

4. If you want to hang the garland vertically, punch a hole in one end shape, thread some ribbon through to make a loop and hang up. To hang it horizontally, punch a hole at either end of the garland, tie ribbon through both holes and hang up.

2a

3

❊ *Gilded* PICTURE FRAME ❊

Gilding is a very old but simple art and gives stunning results. To add a touch of opulence to Iman and Heather's art deco living room, I decided to try my hand at it on their photo frames. As expert Adam Williamson told me, you can gild straight onto wooden frames, as I did here, so long as the wood isn't bare and porous. If it is, apply a primer undercoat before you start.

You will need

1 fine artist's paintbrush

Fast-drying gold size (a type of glue)

Frame (ours was 50 x 40 cm)

Test piece of wood (for testing the tackiness of the size, optional)

1 book of 23-carat gold transfer leaf (24 sheets)

Cotton wool balls

Mop brush

1. Paint the frame with size, applying it as evenly as possible so that it all dries at the same rate. If possible, also paint a test piece of wood (the same wood as your frame). Depending on the size of your frame, leave to dry for 30–60 minutes, or until the size is tacky enough for the gold leaf to stick to it. Test the tackiness by touching the test piece of wood (not the frame itself) with your knuckle – it should feel like Sellotape. If you don't have a test piece of wood, another way to judge that the size is ready is when it looks matt and doesn't reflect light well.

2. Once the size is ready, you can start gilding. Lay the first sheet of gold transfer leaf on the frame and rub the backing lightly with a cotton wool ball until you see it has taken (you will know this because the colour of the gold changes slightly, photo 2a). Very gently, pull off the backing to reveal the gold stuck to the frame (photo 2b). Repeat this step, lining up the gold leaf segment by segment, until the whole frame is covered. Leave the frame to dry overnight.

3. When the frame is dry, use a mop brush to gently remove any excess gold from it. You can then burnish the gold with cotton wool to give it a lovely shine. Start this gently, then press slightly harder to get your desired effect. Put your photographs into the finished frame and display as you wish.

Dip-dyed BASKET

Around the vintage home it's the lovely little extras and special details that add a sprinkling of magic. This idea for dip-dyeing baskets is a simple and easy craft that doesn't take long to do, but produces excellent results. I showed Janine and Shaun how to do this for their *fin de siècle* bedroom (see page 132), and we used white paint, but this craft could be done in a variety of colours and used for almost any vintage room. Try dazzling psychedelic colours for a 1960s' feel, or earthy oranges and greens to complement a 1970s' room.

You will need

Dust sheets or newspaper

White paint (cheap water-based emulsion is best)

Wide plastic tub, for holding paint

Sheet of cardboard, large enough for the dipped basket to stand on

Basket of your choice

Pencil

1. Cover your working area with dust sheets or newspaper.

2. Pour the paint into the plastic tub, then place the sheet of cardboard alongside.

3. Take your basket and decide how high you would like the colour to come. Make a pencil mark at that point, then lower the basket into the paint up to that mark. Lift up the basket and allow as much excess paint as much as possible to drip back into the tub.

4. Stand the basket on the cardboard and leave until it has stopped dripping. Once the dripping has stopped, turn it upside down and leave to dry.

Vintage PINBOARD

A pinboard is a really great addition to a child's bedroom, but you don't want it to be brown and boring. Give it some oomph with vintage fabric to turn it into an eye-catching feature.

You will need

Tape measure

Pinboard

Pencil and paper

Scissors

Wadding (any type will do, but light wadding may need to be doubled to give enough padding)

White fabric, such as calico or something similarly strong

Vintage fabric

Staple gun

Ribbons

Drawing pins

Buttons and/or beads (optional)

1. Measure the length and width of your pinboard and make a note of the measurements. Cut a piece of wadding to exactly the same size.

2. Measure a piece of white fabric and a piece of vintage fabric to your pinboard measurements, adding about another 10 cm on all sides so that the pieces will wrap around the board and can be stapled at the back. Cut them out.

3. Place the wadding on top of the pinboard, lay the white fabric over it, then staple the fabric to the back of the board, pulling it taut as you do so. Use the same process to staple the vintage fabric to the back of the board.

4. To decorate the board, criss-cross it with ribbons, pinning them at the back, and pushing in drawing pins at the intersections on the front. If you prefer, you could stitch buttons and/or beads at these points.

5. Trim off the excess fabric at the back, and cover the raw edges with ribbon, fixing it in place with drawing pins. Photos and cards can simply be tucked behind the ribbon 'grid', making the display easy to change.

3

5

PORTOBELLO
ROAD W11
KENSINGTON AND CHELSEA
LONDON

Pegged ARTWORK

Making a display for your walls is a fantastic way to add a completely personal touch to your room. I'm always banging on about covering your walls with items that reflect you and your family, and here is a really creative and cheap idea that will add a touch of pizazz to your vintage room. All you need is some wire, mini pegs and whatever artwork or vintage finds you want to display.

You will need

Tape measure

Pencil

Jewellery-making craft wire

Scissors

Drill

Wall plugs and corresponding screws

Screwdriver

Mini pegs

Children's art or vintage photographs and postcards – whatever you like

1. Measure the space where you want to string your artwork and mark the wall lightly in pencil to indicate the end points.

2. Measure out the same length of craft wire, adding another 10 cm before you cut it.

3. Drill holes in the wall at the points you marked with pencil. Insert wall plugs and then the corresponding screws. Twist the craft wire around the screws to secure at either end.

4. Now use the mini pegs to clip your chosen artwork, photos or vintage finds along the wire.

VINTAGE
CELEBRATIONS

Being the hostess can be so much fun. I absolutely love it, and I want to share my secrets for creating celebrations that are vintage in every sense of the word.

In the TV series *Kirstie's Vintage Home* I helped an engaged couple, Amy and Craig, to plan and organise their wedding day. It was such a privilege to be involved, and I can tell you now, it was a huge success. They wanted a military theme because Craig serves with the Household Cavalry Regiment, and Amy's family has a military past too – her grandparents were in the army during the Second World War. The 1940s had a special significance, as that is when both sets of grandparents got married, so I thought that would be the perfect era to give the classic elegance Amy craved. Craig's army uniform colours of navy blue, red and gold provided the colour theme, and the result on the day was truly splendid.

There is loads that can be learnt from what we did for the wedding, so read on and you'll discover lots of great ideas that can be tailored to suit your own vintage celebration.

One hard-won word of advice: don't stress yourself out trying for perfection. I always end up giving myself a hard time trying to get everything just right. Remember, your guests are friends and they won't mind the odd hiccup. They'll be too busy having a good time. Happy planning!

START WITH THE DETAILS

Whether you're planning a wedding, a birthday party or a dinner for friends, organising a good party takes meticulous planning, attention to detail and careful preparation. Don't be nervous – it's a wonderful chance to let your creativity flow. Here are a few tips.

INVITATION

The invitations you send out will create the first impression of your party and give the guests some idea of what awaits them. Formal, informal, fancy dress or funny, nothing says care and attention more than a handcrafted invitation landing on the doormat.

My wedding couple, Amy and Craig, made beautiful paper-cut invitations and got a bunch of their family and friends to help them – a great idea if you have lots to make. Poppy Chancellor helped us with a design, incorporating horseshoes and trumpets to reflect both wedding tradition and Craig's army career, and this gave them a regal, vintage feel, as well as making them completely personal (see page 200 to make your own design). If you don't have the time or inclination to make your own, it's possible to buy vintage-inspired invitations in stationery shops and online.

Tradition decrees that invitations (especially wedding invitations) are sent out six to eight weeks before the big day. In recent years, a new tradition has developed, and many people also send out 'save the date' cards up to a year in advance to make sure they bag the date in everyone's diary. These cards don't have to be elaborate or specially printed. You can easily make them yourself and have fun thinking of novel presentation ideas. For example, you might pick up packs of vintage playing cards and stick your message to the suit of hearts cards. Alternatively, paper gift tags have a real vintage feel and look great hand-stamped with the details.

FOOD AND DRINK

When planning your party menu, my advice is to keep it as simple as you can. One of the best ways to do this is to buy local seasonal produce (it ought to be cheaper too). If you are cooking, stick to tried and tested recipes, or do a dummy run before the party so that you discover the tricky bits in advance. Your party is not the occasion to try out new flavours and ideas for the first time. If you do want to experiment, save the results for good friends who won't mind if it doesn't work.

For a real vintage feel to your party, research the type of food that people might have served during your chosen era. For example, nothing says 1970s' dinner party more than prawn cocktails and beef bourguignon!

A buffet is a lovely, relaxed way to feed guests, and the fantastic thing about this option is that a lot of the work can be done in advance, leaving you more time to mingle and enjoy yourself. A buffet can work for all sorts of celebrations, even something formal, such as a wedding. Amy wanted a traditional wedding breakfast, but she saved on costs by having just the starters and mains as served courses. She then had a wonderful dessert table (courtesy of certain relatives and friends, including me, who brought along their favourite puds), where guests could help themselves. It was brilliant and looked sensational (see page 195). I took a summer berry cheesecake, the bridesmaids made an incredible croquembouche (profiterole tower) that took them at least four attempts to get right, parents, aunts, brothers and friends all brought something delicious, and it gave the day another really lovely handmade touch.

[T88]

My top tip for planning your buffet is to make sure you have a great variety of foods on the menu. It's always better to have too much than too little, and there's nothing nicer than getting stuck into the leftovers the next day. (You can find advice about catering quantities in various cookbooks.)

Serving an old-fashioned drink as guests arrive makes a great talking point for a vintage party. At Amy and Craig's wedding I made two types of cocktail: a traditional grenadier cocktail and a twist on the clover club, which I renamed the Shugborough shake after the venue where the wedding was held. We made sure everyone had just one of each (they were quite strong and rather extravagant), and served them alongside traditional canapés, such as smoked salmon blinis and smoked mackerel tartlets. Another brilliant idea is to brew your own beer, which Craig and a couple of his friends did very successfully at a small, local brewery. They even adorned the barrel with a lovely old-fashioned label.

SEATING PLAN

It isn't just at formal events like weddings that a seating plan is a great idea. Any type of sit-down occasion benefits from a seating plan because it ensures the guests mingle – always a good thing.

Think about displaying your plan on the way into your celebration so that guests can find their seats easily. Poppy Chancellor made the most beautiful seating plan for Amy and Craig, which matched the paper-cut invitations that she also designed.

Incidentally, when deciding whether to have a sitting or standing 'do', remember that sitting ensures any vintage theme used to decorate your tables will be properly seen and appreciated.

PLACE CARDS AND SETTINGS

Remember, it's the small details that count: they can have a disproportionately big impact. It isn't difficult to craft beautiful place cards, and they can echo the theme of the invitations and incorporate pretty vintage details. Link them to your place settings too and you're onto a winner. For Amy and Craig's wedding I found vintage ribbon on the Portobello Road to tie little sprays of red and white carnations (the truly vintage blood-and-bandages variety, representative of the battlefields). Each guest's name was written on an old luggage label in beautiful calligraphy, and a gorgeous military button finished each little masterpiece. (See page 196 to make these, or something very similar, for your celebrations.)

Opposite: *The beautiful paper-cut seating plan designed by Poppy Chancellor. Each row of tables was named after a famous racehorse.*

Even if time or money are in short supply, your table can still look wonderful. You might simply write guests' names on a decorative paper doily for a vintage feel; or collect pebbles and write the names on those for a quirky, original look.

HANDMADE DECORATIONS

Do leave plenty of time to make decorations (I think this is one of the best bits about holding a party). Remember that every last detail, from the venue itself right down to the drinks is a potential styling opportunity. None of it has to be expensive. As with styling your home, you can achieve a wonderful look for your celebration with a combination of second-hand shopping and home crafting.

Gather together all your scraps of fabric and make lovely vintage bunting and garlands to hang all around – as far as I'm concerned you can never have too many. Add appliqué to each flag or, even better, monogram each one with embroidered initials – if you have the time. You could also embellish bunting flags with ribbon tassels or small bells that will jingle in the breeze when hung outside.

Garlands too can be handmade from just about anything – paper, fabric, leaves, flowers, ribbon, paper doilies, crochet flowers, glass baubles hung up with string … the list goes on. I made a lovely felt garland to decorate a bedroom on page 174. You could adapt this and use it to add a beautiful finishing touch to your celebration.

Paper decorations can be handmade very cheaply and easily. To make tassel chains, for example, cut lots of thin strips of tissue paper, stack them in bundles and fold the bundles over a length of rope at regular intervals. Grasp both halves of each bundle under the rope and twist the first 5 cm together. Paste the twist with PVA glue, put a peg just below the glued part and leave to dry. Remove the pegs before you hang up the chain. The result is really simple but beautifully effective.

Handmade wooden signs add a marvellous decorative touch, and it doesn't take a carpenter to make them. Just paint your message on pieces of driftwood or any reclaimed wood, or, if you are feeling bold, use a soldering iron to char it onto the surface. Alternatively, collect shells from the beach and glue them onto driftwood as simple decorations.

Amy and Craig's wedding venue was also decorated with lots of willow hearts created by craftsman Eddie Glew (see his technique for making willow placemats on page 170).

Opposite: *Woven willow hearts were decorated with hydrangeas and foliage to tie in visually to the table decorations at the wedding.*

Kirstie's GUIDE TO SETTING A TABLE

I love taking the time to lay a table beautifully for a special occasion. It's a quiet, thoughtful task, and a great opportunity to continue your theme through the whole arrangement. Here are the key things to consider...

Let's start with the base – table linen. I think linen makes the table look warm and inviting. It can be part of a colour theme or add pattern, so please don't dismiss it. Try layering up similar-coloured vintage tablecloths and overlaying them with a lace cloth. Remember, your tablecloth doesn't have to cover the table completely. It will look equally good at an angle.

Consider table runners too. Amy and Craig created gorgeous runners in red and blue cotton for their wedding, which looked amazing running along the length of their dining tables. They went for the rustic, homespun look, but runners can be as sophisticated or festive as you wish.

Don't be too fussy about napkins – they look great whether they match your tablecloth or not. Just make sure you display them beautifully (page 202 shows how to make a napkin rose). For a buffet, pile them onto a tray and put a pretty knick-knack on top to hold them together. Spray-paint your knick-knack to coordinate with your colour scheme (see page 152). Amy and Craig used navy blue ribbon and military buttons to make a 'ring' for each napkin, and put a place card on top, which looked wonderfully pretty (see page196). Adapt this idea to suit your own vintage theme, perhaps by using lace and vintage keys.

Now think about crockery and cutlery. My table settings are usually relaxed because I like everything to be mixed and matched rather than coordinated. Don't feel you must have everything the same. In fact, mixing and matching adds to a vintage, homespun feel. Plus, there is nothing worse than having everything matching and then finding you are missing one piece. With my method this will never happen. It also adds lots of colour and pattern to your table. Second-hand markets, charity shops, junk shops and car boot sales are always packed to the rafters with old crockery, so start your mix and match collection today.

Next add your cutlery, including serving spoons and tongs (if necessary). Give them a good polish before you lay them out because shiny things always look more inviting.

One other point – like my linen, I never keep crockery or cutlery for 'best'. Chances are, if you keep stuff in the sideboard waiting for an extra special occasion, it will never see the light of day. Share and enjoy it.

Don't forget the decorations. Taking the time to decorate your table shows you've put thought and effort into the occasion. For me, this starts with flowers because they really set a table off and make things feel celebratory. Amy and Craig learnt how to decorate a candelabra with flowers for their top table (see page 208 for the technique).

Think creatively about vases. Vintage bottles, cake tins and jelly moulds can make great containers for flowers, and often go for a song at second-markets and shops. For Amy and Craig's wedding table we used vintage pressed glass vases with gold rims that we picked up very cheaply.

Don't feel you have to spend exorbitant amounts on flowers. Use what's in your garden, or forage in the local hedgerows. Amy went out hunting with floral designer Kitten Grayson the day before her wedding to find lavender for her bouquet – everyone was 'digging for victory'! Remember too that greenery and even herbs can make as much of an impact as flowers. Be creative with what's on your doorstep.

Finally, don't forget to put candles on your table. They create a soft and relaxing atmosphere. I like to have a couple of large candles in the middle of the table, and then lots of tea-lights in small containers dotted all over. Make your own vintage-style candle-holders by wrapping lace around jam jars and securing it with adhesive or a stitch (these can work as vases too). It looks so pretty when night falls and there's a tea-light glowing at each table setting.

Kirstie's PARTY CHECKLIST

6–8 WEEKS IN ADVANCE

• Start shopping early: order any cakes, special ingredients or drinks you can get well in advance; starting early also helps to spread the cost of your party.

• Send out invitations.

• Rope in friends and family if you are going to need any extra help on the day.

• Source any extra tables and chairs, if required.

• Start your music playlist.

THE WEEK BEFORE

• Wash your table linen and clean the crockery, glasses and cutlery.

• Make decorations.

• Do any advance cooking (it's a good idea to freeze as much as you can).

TWO DAYS BEFORE

• Clean the house.

• Rearrange the furniture, if required.

• Put away any valuable ornaments or items that might get broken.

• Plan your food timings so that everything can be ready at the same time.

THE DAY BEFORE

• Put up decorations.

• Press your table linen and fully set the table.

• Buy (or forage) flowers and arrange them in containers.

• Buy the fresh food and prepare any dishes that will keep in the fridge.

• Take any frozen dishes out of the freezer.

• Chill drinks.

ON THE DAY

• Do any cooking still required.

• Set out the food if having a buffet.

• Get yourself ready, press play on your music system, pour yourself a drink, relax and enjoy!

Opposite: *Every element of Amy and Craig's wedding came together beautifully and ensured they had a fantastic day.*

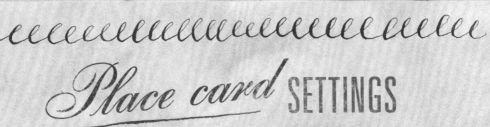

Place card SETTINGS

Making your own place cards for a wedding or celebration is a real opportunity to show off your crafting skills, and the results can really help to bring your theme together with that extra wow factor.

For Amy and Craig's wedding, we used vintage-style baggage labels for the cards and enlisted Claire Gould to write the names on them in beautiful calligraphy (it's cheaper than you might think to hire an expert). To make the place setting, we tied white linen napkins with dark blue ribbon and attached a military button to each one. A carnation and card were then tucked underneath the ribbon. As you can see, the result was absolutely beautiful, and it's easy to tailor to your own celebration.

You will need (per setting)

Linen napkin

2 types of ribbon: one for the napkin, the other for the carnation

Military button (you could also use a brooch or badge)

Needle and thread (optional)

Carnation

Scissors

Long, headed pin

Calligraphy pen (optional)

Baggage label

1. Fold your napkin in half from side to side, then fold into thirds so that you have a narrow rectangle. Wrap or tie a piece of ribbon around it and sew or pin the button or brooch in the centre.

2. Trim the carnation stalk to a length of 3–4 cm. Wrap a 15 cm length of ribbon around the stem. Secure with a long, headed pin at the top.

3. Using a calligraphy pen (or enlisting an expert), write the name of a guest on the baggage label in vintage-style lettering. (If doing this yourself, it's a good idea to practise on scrap paper before attempting it for real.)

4. Tuck the carnation under the ribbon around the napkin, then place the label on top so it covers the stem. Voilà! One stunning place setting.

Paper-cut INVITATIONS

I f you are looking to create a unique party or celebration, the first hint you can give your guests that something special awaits them is via the invitation. Amy and Craig's plan for a vintage wedding needed an invitation that was unlike any other. It had to have a vintage wow factor.

Cue a call to Poppy Chancellor, a designer, illustrator and maker of the most beautiful paper-cuts. She incorporated trumpets and horseshoes into the design for Amy and Craig to reflect their vintage wedding theme and also Craig's work in the army.

If you fancy trying the simple craft of paper cutting, you can tailor Poppy's templates on page 200 to suit your particular celebration. Alternatively, design your own, keeping to simple shapes at first and ensuring that some parts of the design are joined to the outer border of the card to keep it all together. Once you've had some practice, you can build up to more detailed designs.

You will need

Tracing paper and pencil

Small sheets of 160 gsm paper (ours were slightly smaller than A5)

A4 cutting mat, or piece of very thick cardboard

Flat scalpel (we used a 1A blade)

Tri-fold card mounts, with a window cut from the front (you can make these yourself, or buy them ready made)

Glue and/or tape

1. Trace one of Poppy's templates on page 200, then place the tracing face down on a sheet of 160 gsm paper. Using a hard pencil, shade the back of the tracing so that the design transfers to the cutting paper. Remember, it will be a mirror image of the template.

2. Place the paper on the cutting mat and use the scalpel to cut out the shaded areas. It's best to start in the middle and cut outwards. Move the paper rather than the scalpel as you cut, and make lots of short cuts rather than long cuts as these make the scalpel easier to control.

3. Once the cutting is complete, stick the cut-out behind the window of your chosen mount using glue or tape.

1

2

3

Rose NAPKIN

In Victorian times, a creatively folded napkin was an essential part of any dining table, and I'm determined to bring this tradition back to our dining tables today. I adore vintage linen napkins, but this project works with any kind of square napkin, and you can get paper ones with lovely vintage-inspired designs.

1. Place your napkin right side down. Fold each corner into the centre, making sure your creases are flat. Take the new corners and fold them into the centre, then repeat for a third time.

2. Turn the napkin over and fold the corners into the middle on this side (hold them down with the flat of your hand). Now take a corner and fold about 1 cm of it towards the centre. Holding it down, reach underneath and pull up the flap, pushing the folded corner through so that you create a petal shape. Repeat on the remaining three corners.

3. Between each petal that you have created, reach underneath and pull up the flap. Again repeat on each side.

4. Turn the napkin over and you have four more flaps. Pull these out to make the final petals. Repeat the steps to make as many napkin roses as you like.

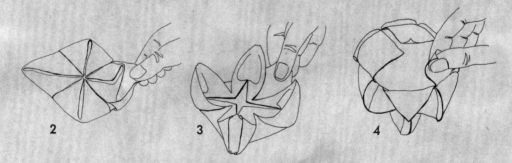

2   3   4

Handmade WEDDING RINGS

Selecting a wedding ring can be a daunting experience. It's a one-off piece of jewellery that you are going to wear for the rest of your life, so it has to have special meaning for you. That's why the trend towards unique handmade designs has become so popular. But where do you start?

Rachel Jeffrey, a contemporary jewellery designer, creates personalised handmade jewellery, and she came along to my vintage café to help Amy and Craig make their wedding rings. The couple wanted to stick with tradition and make really simple, classic rings in white gold that they could have engraved later. They also wanted to make each other's rings to give them extra special meaning.

Not one to miss the party, I joined in by learning how to make a beautiful white gold bangle.

Rachel started making jewellery in her spare room, so it is possible to tackle this project at home (in a well-ventilated room), but it does require specialist equipment, so it's definitely for the committed jeweller, not the beginner. If you want to make your own wedding ring, I suggest you either commission a jeweller to make one for you, or join a jewellery-making class, like those Rachel runs at her jewellery school. (A quick search online should produce a list of jewellers and classes local to you.)

For an added vintage twist, you can reuse old silver or gold to make your rings. All you need is enough to give you the width of the rings plus around 10 cm in length. Your chosen jeweller will be able to advise you about quantity and can melt it down for you.

Here is how Rachel goes about making rings from the basic gold wire.

HEATING THE METAL

The process begins by heating the metal on a heat-resistant mat with a small hand-held blowtorch until it turns a dark cherry-red colour. It is then plunged into cold water to cool it off. This leaves the metal warm enough to be pliable, but cool enough to handle.

SHAPING THE RING

With pliers, the metal is bent into a C-shape, and a mallet is then used to hammer the metal until the ends of the C cross over and there is no gap (photo A). It is then slipped onto a jewellers' ring sizer (known as a 'triblet') to help get the shape and size right (photo B). It can be a very small margin between a ring that fits and one that doesn't. A ring should go smoothly on and off the finger with just a slight wiggle. It can take several attempts to get the size right.

FORMING THE JOIN

Once the size is right, the next step is to saw gently through the ring where the ends cross over. The excess metal will simply drop off. Make sure you keep it as it can be melted down for your next project! The sawn ends must then be realigned to ensure they are parallel and join exactly. This part can be tricky as it requires delicacy to tap the mallet one side at a time and gently close the join.

SOLDERING THE JOIN

When the join is perfect, it is lightly sanded, carefully cleaned, and then soldered together with borax. Once this is done, the ring is plunged into water so it becomes cool again (photo C). At this point, an acidic substance called 'pickle in a pot' is used to clean any excess borax off the ring. When the ring comes out of the pot, it may still not be perfectly round, so it might go back on the triblet and be hammered with the mallet until it is the correct shape.

FINISHING THE RING

The final part of the process is to ensure the best finish on the ring. This starts by filing in one direction to remove any excess solder. Next, a sanding stick is used to sand the whole surface of the ring. After that, a jeweller's electric polisher and specialist polish are used to shine up the metal. Last but not least, the ring is hand-buffed with a special cloth to remove excess polish (photo D).

If the ring has to be stored for a while, Rachel recommends wrapping it in acid-free tissue paper or acid-free velvet to avoid tarnishing, and rubbing it regularly with a polishing cloth to keep it shiny.

A

B

C

D

Flower CANDELABRA

Flowers can make a real statement at a wedding, and you can really set your vintage theme through both your selection of flowers and the way you style them. Amy and Craig wanted a grand table centre on the top table to complement their regal, military theme, and nothing says 'grand' more than a candelabra engulfed by flowers.

Candelabras can readily be picked up in second-hand shops and markets, so keep an eye out, and remember that any wear and tear can often be easily rectified. Also, once you have decorated the candelabra with flowers, the flaws won't show and it will look spectacular. It's like transforming an ugly duckling into a swan.

Weddings are an expensive business, and styling some of your own flowers can save a fortune. All you need are a few insider secrets, so floral designer Kitten Grayson came along to give the happy couple and me a lesson. Her best tip was to use lots of foliage as a cheap and effective way to create the base for a large arrangement. That way the flowers you do spend money on will stand out to full effect. Kitten used berried ivy in this arrangement for its romantic qualities and also because it's freely available around the countryside and in gardens. That's another tip: always look on your doorstep for foliage and flowers for your own personal arrangement, and if you do buy flowers, save money by choosing those that are in season.

You will need

Florist's foam (the amount needed depends on the size of your candelabra – see step 1)

Scissors or sharp knife

Candelabra

Florist's tape

Selection of foliage and flowers (we used two types of ivy – one with berries, and frothy *Alchemilla mollis* for greenery, viburnum berries, unripe blackberries, hydrangeas, pink roses, red carnations, purple scabious, lavender, and mauve and magenta sweetpeas)

Candles

1. Soak the florist's foam in water for at least 30 minutes, allowing the water to sink in naturally rather than forcing it. This way it draws up the water evenly.

2. Once the foam is completely soaked through, cut it into equal pieces and wedge them between the branches of the candelabra.

3. Use florist's tape to fix the foam so that it doesn't move. You don't have to be neat because it will be eventually covered with flowers. Simply wind the tape around as many times as it takes to form a really secure base for the arrangement. You might want to enlist an extra pair of hands to help you with this.

4. Now it's time to start inserting stems into the foam, but first a word of warning: if you remove a stem from a hole, that hole cannot be reused because the cells have been crushed and will not allow the stem to take up water effectively, so think things through before plunging in. Beginning with the ivy, cut the stems at an angle, then insert them into the foam, starting at the bottom and placing them at an angle. This helps to keep them secure and allows them to take up water effectively. As you progress, take a step back and move around the candelabra, assessing how it looks overall.

5. Once you have covered the foam with ivy, add the berries next, spacing them evenly throughout the arrangement. Now do the same with the *Alchemilla mollis*.

6. The flowers come next. Cut each stem to the required length (10–20 cm, depending on how far out you want it to stand) just before adding it to the arrangement – you need to judge each one. Also, cut the stems at an angle to help the flowers take up water. Start with the larger ones – we began with three stems of hydrangea because they really fill the space. After that we added roses, carnations, scabious, lavender and sweetpeas (in that order) evenly throughout the arrangement. Kitten recommends placing the flowers in groups of three because this gives the arrangement balance and is more akin to how flowers grow in the wild. Keep taking a step back and checking that you are happy with how the arrangement looks.

7. Finally, insert candles in the candelabra and place the arrangement on the table for all to admire.

Wedding BUTTONHOLES

Floral designer Kitten Grayson showed me how to make lovely wedding buttonholes, which traditionally match the bride's bouquet. Amy and Craig added military buttons for a personal touch, and you could add vintage buttons too if you wish. Ideally, make your buttonholes on the day of the wedding. If not, make them the day before and keep them in the fridge.

You will need

Selection of flowers and greenery – we used roses, sprigs of unripe blackberries, hydrangea, lavender and frothy *Alchemilla mollis*)

Scissors

Florist's wire

Florist's paper gutter tape

Ribbon (10–15 cm per buttonhole, depending on the width of the ribbon)

Small straight pins

Needle and thread (optional)

Buttons (optional)

Long pearl-headed pins

1. Start by cutting the stems of the flowers, foliage and berries for one buttonhole: those at the back should be about 4 cm long, and those at the front about 2 cm, so experiment to find an arrangement you like.

2. Now you have to wire each stem to provide more structure. To do this, take a piece of florist's wire double the length of the stem, fold it in half and place the looped end around the top of the stem (photo 2a). Holding it in place there, wrap the wire around the stem all the way to the bottom (photo 2b). If working with thick stems, such as roses, you can simply push the wire into them until it breaks through the top. Don't go too far – it will feel soft.

3. Wrap florist's tape around each wired stem all the way down. Group the arrangement as you want it, starting with a rose, then adding the berries, other flowers and foliage. Hold the bunch firmly and, starting at the top, bind the tape tightly around the stems, overlapping it as you go.

4. Now wrap your chosen colour of ribbon around the stems to cover all the tape. Secure in place with a small pin, then sew a button onto it if you wish.

5. The buttonhole can now be pinned to the left lapel of a man's jacket with a pearl-headed pin either from the front or the back (the choice is yours).

2a

2b

Contact LIST

CONTRIBUTORS

Here is a list of all the talented and wonderful craftspeople who contributed their designs, craft expertise and enthusiasm to *Kirstie's Vintage Home*.

Simon Bell
www.voutique.co.uk/last-place-on-earth
An expert in furniture upcycling, Simon taught me how to distress chairs and reupholster the seats that looked fabulous in Janine and Shaun's 1950s' playroom (pages 66 and 115).

Poppy Chancellor
http://poppychancellor.com
Poppy is a talented paper artist, and designed the beautiful, personal wedding invitations on page 198. She also designed and cut the seating plan for Amy and Craig's big day (page 188).

Lisa Comfort
http://sewoverit.co.uk
Sewing expert and teacher Lisa runs classes from her sewing café, Sew Over It. She took Amber and Colin through the quilting process (page 108) and also made the baby changing mat (page 120).

Jessie Ford
www.jessieford.co.uk and www.sugarsnapstudio.co.uk
Jessie is a talented illustrator who created all the look books that brought together each family's ideas and inspirations for their vintage makeovers. See page 51 for an example of her work.

Anselm Fraser
www.anselmfraser.com and www.chippendale.co.uk
Furniture designer and restoration expert Anselm runs the Chippendale Furniture School, and he showed Janine and Shaun how to make the wooden treasure chest on page 70.

Eddie Glew

www.blithfieldwillowcrafts.co.uk
Willow weaver Eddie learnt all his skills from his father, and now runs Blithfield Willow Crafts, where he teaches workshops. He taught Ellie, Nick and me how to make willow placemats and also provided a selection of beautiful willow hearts and decorations for Amy and Craig's wedding (pages 170 and 191).

Claire Gould

www.calligraphy-for-weddings.com
Expert calligrapher Claire did all the beautiful writing for the name place settings (page 196).

Kitten Grayson

www.kittengrayson.com
Floral designer Kitten showed Amy, Craig and me how to make stunning candelabra arrangements (page 208) and beautiful buttonholes (page 212). Her expertise truly made the couple's wedding extra special.

Rachel Jeffrey

www.racheljeffrey.co.uk
As a goldsmith and silversmith, Rachel has undertaken commissions for the royal family, so Amy and Craig were honoured to have her teach them how to make their very own wedding rings (page 204).

Richard Miller

www.richmiller.co.uk and www.froyles.com
Richard is an ace potter who came to my vintage HQ to show Ellie and Nick how to make hand-moulded plates (page 160). He also provided handmade bespoke tiles for their kitchen splashback (page 166).

Zoe Murphy

http://www.zoemurphy.com
Designer Zoe specialises in bespoke furniture and textiles. Upcycling interior pieces is her passion, and she helped Amber and Colin to transform the sideboard for their 1960s' sitting room (page 80).

Junior Phipps

www.consciousforms.com
Furniture and product designer Junior is an expert in 3D design. He does amazing things with concrete, and also designed a tree mural for Richard and his daughters (page 86).

Selina Rose

www.selinarose.co.uk
Award-winning designer and maker Selina creates intricately cut felt homewares. She made a stunning felt rug for Amy and Daisy's bedroom (page 104).

Zeena Shah

www.zeenashah.com
Homeware and textile designer Zeena taught me lino-cut printing to decorate a pretty blind for Ellie and Nick's kitchen (page 124), as well as how to make novelty cushions for Iman and Heather (page 128). She also runs workshops.

Sue Timney

www.suetimney.com
Sue is a renowned textile expert and interior designer who created the stunning wedding canopy (page 132) and the quirky crochet jellyfish (page 154).

Adam Williamson

www.adamwilliamson.com
Adam is a stone and wood carver, but also a specialist in the ancient art of gilding. He teaches these skills (amongst many others) at his workshops, and showed me how to gild with gold leaf (page 177).

SHOPS AND ANTIQUES CENTRES

Here is a list of the places where I took our participating families to look for vintage treasures and bargains for their makeovers.

Chic Antique
www.chicantique.co.uk
I popped into this Isle of Wight shop with Richard for a spot of second-hand shopping for his 1970s' makeover.

The Cloth Shop
www.theclothshop.net
Based in London's Portobello Road, the Cloth Shop is an Aladdin's cave of everything to do with fabric. What owners Sam and Alex don't know about their specialism just isn't worth knowing!

Last Place on Earth
http://lastplaceonearth.co.uk
This wonderful shop was next door to my vintage HQ in Portobello Road, and is packed full of everything from quality antique furniture, mirrors and lights to vintage letters.

Newbury IACF International Antiques and Collectors Fair
www.iacf.co.uk/newbury
The Newbury Antiques Fair in Berkshire is second-hand shopping heaven. It has literally hundreds of stalls and thousands of vintage items to bargain for.

Park Royal Salvage
www.parkroyalsalvage.co.uk
I'm a regular at Ray Cullop's salvage yard in west London, and I took some of the families along to shop there. It's a real treasure trove and well worth a visit.

Portobello and Golbourne Markets
http://shopportobello.co.uk and www.portobelloroad.co.uk
These are my absolute favourite markets, where I could spend oodles of time shopping, browsing and bargaining for vintage treasures.

PROPS AND SERVICES

During the course of the TV series, many companies and individuals gave very generously of their time and products, and we are hugely grateful.

Jane Beck
http://welshblankets.co.uk
The ultimate in comfort is a beautiful Welsh blanket, as sold by Jane Beck.

Chic Concept
www.chicconcept.co.uk
If you're desperate for a starburst mirror to complete your 1960s' makeover, look no further than Chic Concept, which provided the stunning gold mirror in Amber and Colin's sitting room (page 46).

Collingwood Lighting Group
www.collingwoodlighting.com
Recommended by 3D designer Junior Phipps, Collingwood is an excellent source of light fittings and components.

Demi's Florist
www.demisflowers.co.uk
You can see some of the beautiful flowers supplied by Demi on pages 14 and 46.

The Fine Cotton Company
www.thefinecottoncompany.com
If 100% organic cotton bed linen is your thing, this is the company that can supply it.

Jane Foster
www.janefoster.co.uk
Jane supplied vintage barkcloth cushions (page 46) and some of the fabrics used in the 1970s' patchwork (page 49).

Johnstones Paint
www.johnstonespaint.com
The paint produced by this long-established British company is a favourite with professional decorators. It was used in all our room makeovers.

Nina Koenig
www.bagsoflove.co.uk
Nina's company specialises in printing photographs onto a wide variety of surfaces, including fabric. It printed the image that Amber and Colin used on the central square of their quilt (page 109).

Little Greene
www.littlegreene.com
If you need paint in vintage colours, Little Greene can supply it. We used Slaked Lime 105 in the sitting room on page 46.

Mandors
www.mandors.co.uk/contact-mandors-fabric-store.php
This fantastic fabric store in Glasgow was the source of the beautiful fabric used in Amber and Colin's patchwork quilt (page 109).

Ian Mankin
www.ianmankin.co.uk
This company offers a terrific range of fabrics at very competitive prices. It's where we got the materials for the striped blind and cushion on page 109.

Mini Moderns
http://minimoderns.bigcartel.com
A fantastic source of porcelain, cushions and wallpaper inspired by Festival of Britain designs. The beautiful wallpapers used in the bedrooms (pages 49 and 109) both come from this company.

mydeco.com
http://mydeco.com
A fantastic source of furniture and furnishings. I'm a great fan of their cushions, like the Flower Trail design used on the desk chair, page 81.

Garry Olver Painters
yvonne.olver@sky.com
Garry and his cohorts did a great job of painting the rooms on pages 46 and 109.

Original BTC
www.originalbtc.com
This British company is a great source of elegant yet affordable lighting, like the Paxo pendant light on page 109.

Plantation Rug Company
www.plantationrug.co.uk
'Fashion for your floor' is the motto of this company, and it's spot on.

Roberts Radio
www.robertsradio.co.uk
A long-established British company that makes a superb range of radios, including a funky retro design (pages 14 and 125).

Sanderson
http://www.sanderson-uk.com
I've always loved Sanderson fabrics, and their fabulous mustard and red design called Perpetua (part of their 1950s' collection) was used on page 46.

Sofa & Stuff
www.sofasandstuff.com
Want a romantic kingsize bed like Janine and Shaun's (page 133)? This company can supply it.

INDEX

Amber and Colin 14, 46–7
  appliqué quilt 108–13
  handles 63
  look book 50, 51
  mirrors 147
  patchwork quilt 96
  rejuvenated ottoman 74–5
  screen-printed sideboard 19, 80–5
  spray-painting objects 152–3
Amy and Craig 186
  buttonholes 212–13
  flower candelabra 208–11
  food and drink 187, 189
  invitations 186–7, 198–201
  marquee 195
  place cards and settings 189, 196–7
  seating plan 189
  table decorations 192, 193
  wedding rings 204–7
  willow hearts 190, 191
appliqué quilt 108–13
art deco 21, 33–7
  gilded picture frame 176–7
auction houses 16, 18

baby changing mat 120–3
Bakelite 37
basketry: willow placemats 170–3
baskets 149
  dip-dyed basket 178–9
bedrooms: Amber and Colin 46–7
  Daisy and Amy 48–9
  furniture 54
  Janine and Shaun 29
beds 23
  wedding veil canopy 132–7
bedside cabinets 76–7
bedside tables 149
Bell, Simon 66, 114, 218
blinds: lino-cut blind 124–7
bottles: spray-painting 152–3
boxes: trinket boxes 150–1

buffets 187, 189, 192
bunting 190
buttonholes 212–13

cabinets 144
  bedside 76–7
café curtains 99
candles 193
canopies: wedding veil canopy 132–7
celebrations see parties
chairs: distressing 66–9
  folding chairs 99
  reupholstered drop-in seat pad 114–19
Chancellor, Poppy 186, 189, 198, 218
changing mat 120–3
Charles, Prince 98
Cliff, Clarice 160
coffee tables 144, 147
collections 141–3
  how to display 143–7
  colours: 1920s 33
    1930s 39
    1950s 40
    1960s 47
    1970s 49
  colour chart 16
  furniture 61
  room planning 26
Comfort, Lisa 108, 120, 218
Cooper, Susie 160
crocheted jellyfish 154–9
crockery 192–3
curtains 99, 102
cushions 99, 102
  novelty cushion 128–31
cutlery 192–3

Daisy and Amy 48–9
  felt garland 174–5
  punched felt rug 104–7
  tree mural with shelves 86–91
  trinket boxes 150–1
  vintage pinboard 180–1
découpage 63

dip-dyed basket 178–9
director's chairs 99
displays 143–4
  coffee tables 144, 147
  everyday items 149
  pictures 147–8
  shelves and cabinets 144
  walls 147
distressed chair 66–9
DIY toolkit 65
dovetail joints 58
dressing tables 62
drop-in seat pad 114–19
dyeing 132

Ellie and Nick 21, 29, 38–9
  collection 145
  hand-moulded plate 160–5
  handles 63
  lino-cut blind 124–7
  tiled splashback 166–9
  willow placemats 170–3

fabrics: 1950s 40
  choosing 95–6
  cleaning 96, 98
  dyeing 132
  pattern repeat 96
  using 98–100
  washability 96
  weight and durability 96
  where to find 94–5
  width 96
family rooms 40–2, 56, 57
felt garland 174–5
felt rug 104–7
Festival of Britain 40, 42
fin de siècle 29
  bedside cabinets 76–7
  dip-dyed basket 178–9
  memory box 78–9
  wedding veil canopy 132–7
finishing touches 140
  crocheted jellyfish 154–9
  dip-dyed basket 178–9
  displaying everyday items 149
  felt garland 174–5

gilded picture frame 176–7
hand-moulded plate 160–5
hanging pictures 147–8
how to display collections
  143–7
how to put it all together
  140–1
pegged artwork 182–3
spray-painting objects 152–3
tiled splashback 166–9
trinket boxes 150–1
vintage pinboard 180–1
what to display 141–3
willow placemats 170–3
Flight, Claude 124
flowers 193
  flower candelabra 208–11
  wedding buttonholes 212–13
folding chairs 99
Ford, Jessie 214, 218
Fraser, Anselm 70, 218
furniture 54
  1920s 34
  1950s 42
  1960s 47
  1970s 49
  buying 16, 56–60
  choosing 55
  cleaning 60–1
  combining vintage styles 56
  DIY toolkit 65
  reinventing 61–3
  room planning 25–6
  vintage trends and prices 60
  what to buy 54–5

garlands 190
  felt garland 174–5
gilded picture frame 37,
  176–7
glass: art deco 37
  tabletops 63
Glew, Eddie 170, 190, 218
gold leaf gilding 37, 176–7
Gould, Claire 196, 218
Grayson, Kitten 193, 208, 218

half curtains 99
handles 63

Iman and Heather 21, 34–5,
  37
  gilded picture frame 176–7
  novelty cushion 99, 128–31
Internet: auction house
catalogues 18
  auction sites 19
invitations 186–7, 198–201
Janine and Shaun 29, 40–2,
  56, 57
  bedside cabinets 76–7
  dip-dyed basket 178–9
  distressed chair 66–9
  dressing table 62
  look book 50
  memory box 78–9
  reupholstered drop-in seat
pad 114–19
  wedding veil canopy 132–7
  wooden treasure chest 70–3
Jeffrey, Rachel 204, 218
jellyfish 154–9
job lots 18
joints 58

kitchens: 1930s 37–9
  furniture 54
  tiled splashback 166–9

layering 100, 102
lighting: 1960s 47
  art deco 37
  room planning 26
lino-cut blind 39, 124–7
living rooms: 1960s 46–7
  art deco 34, 37
  furniture 54, 149
look books 50–1

markets 21, 219
memory box 78–9
Miller, Richard 160, 167, 218
mirror glass 63

mirrors 147
  1960s 47
  art deco 37
mortise and tenon joints 58
murals: tree mural with shelves
  86–91
Murphy, Zoe 80, 218

napkins 192
  napkin rose 20–3
negotiation 23
novelty cushion 128–31

ottoman 74–5

painting: distressed chair 66–9
  furniture 61
  spray-painting objects 152–3
paper-cut invitations 198–201
parties 186
  checklist 194
  food and drink 187, 189
  handmade decorations
    190–1
  invitations 186–7, 189–201
  napkin rose 20–3
  place cards and settings
    189–90, 196–7
  seating plan 189
  setting a table 192–3
  see also weddings
patchwork 99
  appliqué quilt 108–13
patterns: layering 102
  room planning 26
  swatch 16
pegged artwork 182–3
Phipps, Junior 86, 218
pictures: gilded picture frame
  176–7
  hanging 147–8
pinboard 180–1
place cards and settings
  189–90, 196–7
placemats: willow placemats
  170–3
planning 25–7

plates: hand-moulded plate
    160–5
playrooms 40–2, 56, 57
pottery 39
    hand-moulded plate 160–5

quilts: appliqué quilt 108–13

reclamation yards 21
rings: wedding rings 204–7
room planning 25–7
Rose, Selina 104, 174, 218
rugs 102
    punched felt rug 104–7

Sale of Goods Act 19
salvage yards 21, 219
screen-printed sideboard 80–5
seat pad 114–19
second-hand see vintage
sewing kit 100
Shah, Zeena 124, 128, 218
Shaun and Janine see Janine
    and Shaun
shelves: displays 144
    tree mural with shelves
        86–91
shopping 16–23
sideboards: screen-printed
sideboard 80–5
silk-screen printing 63, 80–5
sitting rooms see living rooms
skips 21
soft furnishings 94
    appliqué quilt 108–13
    arranging 100, 102
    baby changing mat 120–3
    lino-cut blind 124–7
    novelty cushion 128–31
    punched felt rug 104–7
    reupholstered drop-in seat
        pad 114–19
    room planning 26
    sewing kit 100
    wedding veil canopy 132–7
splashback 166–9
spray-painting objects 152–3

tables: bedside 149
    displays 144, 147
    flower candelabra 208–11
    napkin rose 20–3
    place cards and settings
        189–90, 196–7
    setting 192–3
tassel chains 190
throws 102
tiles 39
    tiled splashback 166–9
Timney, Sue 132, 154, 219
tissue boxes 149
toolkits: DIY 65
treasure chest 70–3
tree mural with shelves 86–91
trinket boxes 150–1

upcycling 77
upholstered furniture: buying
    56, 58, 59
    cleaning 61
    layering 100, 102

vases 193
    spray-painting objects 152–3
veneers 63
vintage 12–13
    buying 15–21
    merging old and new 13–15
    personal style 27–9
    shopping guide 22–3
vintage fabrics see fabrics
vintage furniture see furniture
vintage styles 32
    1920s 33–5, 37
    1930s 36, 37–9
    1950s 40–3
    1960s 44–7
    1970s 48–9
    combining 56
    look books 50
    twentieth-century homes
        32–3

wallpaper 63
    tree mural with shelves
        86–91

walls: displays 147
    how to hang pictures 147–8
    pegged artwork 182–3
    room planning 27
    tiled splashback 166–9
water damage 59
wedding rings 204–7
wedding veil canopy 132–7
weddings 186
    buttonholes 212–13
    flower candelabra 208–11
    food and drink 187, 189
    handmade decorations 190–1
    handmade wedding rings
        204–7
    invitations 186–7, 198–201
    place cards and settings 189,
        196–7
    seating plan 189
Williamson, Adam 37, 177, 219
willow hearts 190, 191
willow placemats 170–3
wooden furniture: buying 56,
    58, 59
    cleaning 61
    painting 61
wooden treasure chest 70–3
woodworm 59

ACKNOWLEDGEMENTS

Neither the TV programme nor this book would have been possible without the hard work and talents of so many brilliant craftspeople, and this time I wasn't the only one benefiting from their expertise. I'm thankful to our wonderful home-owners and our first-ever bride and groom, who had faith in our ideas to make their homes and very special day a huge success.

At the centre of it all was my handmade HQ, Kirstie's Vintage Home, a dream workshop made to inspire crafting and creativity across the country. Thanks to Dave Eaton, who shipped out and let us move in to do the filming, and to Jamie Stimpson, who begged, borrowed and bought so many beautiful things from kind people and suppliers to decorate the space. Then there were the amazing Portobello Road residents and helpers, who welcomed us and never said no: Alex and Alice at The Cloth Shop, Harry Hoffen our builder, Simon Bell from next door, Portobello Art and Stationers, and all the neighbours and stallholders who let us film. Not to mention Robert Henry, our barista from Another Cup, who taught me the real art of coffee-making, and the delicious cakes from Beas of Bloomsbury, Patisserie Valerie, Lola's Cupcakes and Hummingbird that we all ate far too many of. Thank you also to all those talented and tolerant folk who crafted so quietly while we filmed, and who waited patiently for us to 'cut' before they could enjoy their cake and coffee.

On the TV front, Sarah Walmsley and Lisa McCann are my driving forces, along with Jane Muirhead, who steers the big ship at Raise the Roof. They are the best team in the world, who don't just make brilliant programmes and beautiful homes, but now create the most exquisite weddings too. Thanks to Dani Carlaw, Ellie De Court, Laura Harding, Janine Finlay, Sandy Whyte, Louise Scrivens, Andrew Walmsley, Nina Brown, Megan Gerrie, Martin Connery, Warren Baxter, Jim Dunbar, Richard Poet, Simon Hamilton, Kate Wilson, Harriette Arthur, Joffa Hardy, Laura Wiseman, Louise McGregor, Katie Buckland, Elaine Walsh, Ann MacDonald, Kirsty MacFarlane, Michael Hunter, Martin Graham, Kevin Walker, Claire Glasgow, Marianne Palmer, Emmily Marshall, Chehvani Leonard, Edwina Boase, Nikki Bradley, Emma Lamp, Jessie Ford, Cliff Evans, Jon Boast, Tim Pitot, Ed Bulman and Andy Allen.

Thanks to Newbury Racecourse and Antiques Fair, who kindly let us film, and to Lynsey Jean Henderson, for letting us into your lovely screen-printing studio.

I am hugely grateful to the Channel 4 team – Andrew Jackson, Karoline Copping, Kate Teckman, Clemency Green, Hanna Warren and Jay Hunt – who keep coming back for more! I'm so glad you do.

To Jeannot Hutcheson and Fiona Murray – two of the loveliest people I know, both patient and kind, talented and incredibly hard-working, and to Janice Walmsley, who has gone above and beyond – thank you.

I am also very grateful to Nicky Ross, Trish Burgess, Sarah Hammond, Leni Lawrence, Georgia Vaux and the team at Hodder, who get involved in the TV madness and pull through it every time.

I truly believe my agent Hilary at Arlington Enterprises is superhuman; and the home team of Beth, Jamie, Heather, Maravic, Angelina, Chrissie and Sophie, you are all heroes.

Finally, thanks to my family, Ben and the boys, who bring me so much pleasure and joy every day – you inspire me in everything I do.

PUBLISHER'S ACKNOWLEDGEMENT
We would like to thank Fiona Murray for her photography.

First published in Great Britain in 2012
by Hodder & Stoughton
An Hachette UK company

2

Copyright © RTRP 2012

A CIP catalogue record for this title is available from the
British Library

Tpbk ISBN 978 1 444 73780 6
Ebook ISBN 978 1 444 7 5804 7

Photography © RTRP 2012

Additional sources: © Andreas von Einsiedel/Alamy
pages 24, 28, 45. © SliceofLondonLife/Alamy page 43.
© Wales Heritage Photos/Alamy page 36. © Elizabeth
Whiting & Associates/Alamy page 35.

Text editor: Jeannot Hutcheson

Project editor: Patricia Burgess
Decorative illustrations: Mark Hearld
Technical illustrations: Polly Webb-Wilson

Designed by Georgia Vaux

Typeset in Fournier and Metalophile

Printed and bound in Germany by Firmengruppe APPL

Hodder & Stoughton policy is to use papers that are
natural, renewable and recyclable products and made
from wood grown in sustainable forests. The logging
and manufacturing processes are expected to conform to
the environmental regulations of the country of origin.

Hodder & Stoughton Publishers
Carmelite House
50 Victoria Embankment
London EC4Y 0DZ

www.hodder.co.uk

MIX
Paper from
responsible sources
FSC® C023561

To the tall one and the small one and all the other
people who have worked on the craft shows —
this is your achievement. And to Rory, Mark and
Andrew — your mum has the patience of a saint.